This book should be returned to any branch of the
Lancashire County Library on or before the date

12 JUL 2012

-8 MAR 2013

30 JUL 2013

19 AUG 2013

29 DEC 2014

-6 JAN 2015

26 JAN 2015

-4 APR 2015

10 OCT 2015

04 FEB 2016

11 APR 2016

10/11/16

08 MAY 2018

28 JAN 2019

10 FEB 2020

NKN

Mountain Views

A lifetime's enjoyment

Mountain
Views

A lifetime's enjoyment

Rupert Hoare

VERTEBRATE PUBLISHING

Vertebrate Publishing, Sheffield
www.v-publishing.co.uk

MOUNTAIN VIEWS: A LIFETIME'S ENJOYMENT

First published in 2011 by Vertebrate Publishing, an imprint of Vertebrate Graphics Ltd.
© Rupert Hoare 2011.

British Library Cataloguing in Publication Data
Hoare, Rupert, 1956–
Mountain Views: A lifetime's enjoyment
1. Mountaineering – Biographies

ISBN 978-1-906148-33-1

This book is a work of non-fiction based on the life, experiences and recollections
of Rupert Hoare. The author has stated to the publishers that, except in such minor respects
not affecting the substantial accuracy of the work, the contents of the book are true.

Every effort has been made to obtain the necessary permissions with
reference to copyright material, both illustrative and quoted.
We apologise for any omissions in this respect and will be pleased to make the
appropriate acknowledgements in any future edition.

Designed and typeset in Arno Pro and Museo by Nathan Ryder – Vertebrate Graphics Ltd. – www.v-graphics.co.uk

Printed and bound in China on behalf of Latitude Press

CONTENTS

Photo opposite: Clocher du Tacul and Mont Blanc.

PREFACE

Saturday 29th January, 2011: My friend Ken White and I are descending Stob a'Choire Mheadhoin in mid-afternoon, one of a pair of Munros known as the 'Easains' on the west side of Loch Treig, in the Western Highlands of Scotland. We have reached a long, level stretch of ridge at about 700m, just below the snowline. Although the morning was cloudy, the weather has cleared to give a stunningly beautiful winter afternoon. The hillside glows orange in the low sun, small patches of cloud linger in the valley and there is a great view of the snowy Creag Meagaidh massif opposite. But my eyes are full of tears. Two days earlier I had been diagnosed with pancreatic cancer.

Pancreatic cancer is the tenth most common cancer and approximately 7000 people in the United Kingdom are diagnosed each year. Survival rates are very poor and I was well aware that Stob a'Choire Mheadhoin might be my last Munro, although I now had only sixteen left to climb out of the total of two hundred and eighty-three.

Hill walking, rock climbing, Alpine mountaineering and ski-mountaineering have been an integral part of my life for the last thirty-eight years. I have never climbed at a very high standard, although some of my Alpine routes have seemed challenging enough. Generally I have found the surroundings and company more important than the grade. This book is an attempt to share some of the beauty and joy from all those precious times.

Those who have shared my mountain days will know that I am not always the most patient companion. This book, too, is written in some haste but this time, with short life-expectancy, perhaps I have more of an excuse. I am fortunate to have kept detailed diaries of every trip, from my very first mountains on the Isle of Jura onwards, and I have used these extensively while writing. I have had to be selective and I have chosen to focus more on earlier trips as they were the most memorable.

Photography has always been very important to me, from my earliest climbs. I love trying to capture an image of the beauty I see in nature. For me, a no-photograph day is usually a poor day. A key objective of this book is to share some of my favourite mountain pictures.

My career in oil-exploration has taken me to some very un-mountainous places such as the deserts of Libya, Central Australia and Pakistan. I have included some pages on these travels as, at times, deserts share qualities of beauty, adventure and wilderness with mountains.

I wish to thank all my companions in the hills over the years and in particular Robert Whitcombe, Philip Tibbs, John Gunner, Simon Mumford, John Davis, Alan Winton, John Evans, John Harding, Derek Fordham, Ken White, and Alison Graham.

I also pay tribute to my parents for their support and encouragement. This is not a full biography but happy family weekends between all the climbing trips have been an important part of my life.

Most of all, I wish to thank my wife Jay for a happy marriage, constant love and twenty-five years of wonderful mountain holidays together.

On Stob a'Choire Mheadhoin, probably my last Munro. *Photo K. White.*

PART 1
The Early Years

"Fortunate indeed is man that he can forget so soon the physical stresses of life and remember only the greater blessings of his strenuous endeavours."

F.S. SMYTHE, IN **THE VALLEY OF FLOWERS**, *1938*

Photo opposite: Robin Thornedyke on The Arête at Garston Rocks.

ONE

First Steps

Winchester

I discovered mountains through books. Two books, from the house library at Winchester College, were responsible. The first was *Annapurna* by Maurice Herzog, which describes the French expedition in 1950. Attempting the first ascent of this 8000m peak, the team's initial challenge was to find the mountain, which took weeks of exploration. Then, after a supreme effort, Herzog and Lachenal reached the summit, followed by a terrible ordeal on the descent, supported by Lionel Terray and Gaston Rébuffat. Despite the gruesome amputation of frostbitten fingers and toes, to an impressionable teenager it sounded a heroic adventure.

I looked for similar books and found *The Romance of Mountaineering* by R L G Irving. Irving was once a teacher – or don, as they are called – at Winchester and was responsible for introducing George Leigh Mallory to the mountains. Nowadays some of the writing seems dated but for me, at the time, the book lived up to its title and really did make mountaineering romantic. I was particularly thrilled by the many black and white plates, each protected by a thin translucent sheet, and especially the rock-climbing photographs. Looking up at the tower of the College chapel, I wondered how people had the nerve to climb vertical rock.

Hooked, I moved on to the city library where there were shelves of mountaineering books which I devoured one after another. Just two remain in my memory, both poignant tragedies: *The Mountain of My Fear* by David Roberts and *The Last Blue Mountain* by Ralph Barker. At about this time, too, my parents gave me the Penguin book *Mountaineering* by Alan Blackshaw and this became my bible, read and re-read.

The dons at Winchester were excellent at encouraging and supporting any interest or enthusiasm. In May 1973, John Hunter Durran, who taught mathematics and was active in the Combined Cadet Force (CCF), took three of us down to Swanage in his ancient Land Rover. The others were my great friend Robert Whitcombe, who started in the same house on the same day, and another pupil James Scott. We walked to an area called Cattle Troughs and learnt how to abseil the classic way, using a hawser-laid rope between the legs and over the shoulder. The climbs we top-roped were extremely easy but seemed exciting at the time and I loved the setting just above the waves and the whole feeling of adventure.

Two months later at CCF camp in Kintyre, I did some more rock climbing and on Jura I reached the top of my first mountain. There is always a special magic about walking and climbing in the Hebridean islands, with the blue sea below, and as we walked up Beinn a'Chaolais, in our prickly army clothing, I couldn't believe the sensation of gaining so much height. (I also learnt about false summits for the first time: there was one after another...) We descended to our camp, observing a beautiful West Coast sunset: natural beauty was already exerting a powerful influence on me.

Later that summer Robert and I set off along the South Downs Way. We only made it about half-way from Eastbourne to Petersfield, for the hard chalk and uncomfortable army boots caused bad blisters. Foolishly, too, we had carried tinned food for the whole journey, as well as our camping equipment, which was quite unnecessary as the route passes close to villages most days. But we had taken our first independent steps outside the auspices of the school CCF.

By December I had acquired a bright orange 'Blacks' anorak. In a CCF group, we made an exciting traverse of the Brecon Beacons from Pen-Twyn to Cwm-llwch and, the next day, walked along a ridge in the Black Mountains in the rain. I found the compass work exciting. Despite getting soaked, I leapt the peat hags from tussock to tussock, feeling a fierce sense of exhilaration, although others were complaining.

Back at school, I noticed an advertisement for a British Schools Exploring Society expedition to Arctic Norway. It sounded a wonderful opportunity, particularly as the expedition included scientific fieldwork and, with my growing interest in mountains, I had chosen to study geology at university. After an interview in London I was offered a place on the expedition.

Before leaving Winchester another don, Tony Ayres, a physicist, took James Scott and me to the Peak District over a spring weekend. The weather was fine, we camped at Hope and climbed at Stanage, top-roping Diffs and V Diffs and enjoying the unique gritstone architecture and fine outlook for the first of so many times. According to my diary, we did thirteen routes the first day, and the next day I got gripped for the first time on a route called Robin Hood's Right Hand Buttress Direct (now graded Hard Severe).

In July, shortly before heading off to Norway, I completed the South Downs Way with another friend, Philip Tibbs. By now I had more comfortable boots, made by Robert Lawrie, a Bukta Orienteer tent and a Karrimor packframe rucksack. They made the trip a great deal easier and more enjoyable and, I hoped, improved my fitness for the forthcoming expedition. Philip, like Robert Whitcombe, was to remain a close friend for the rest of my life. We all three still meet once a year for a walking weekend in the Scottish Highlands. Philip is now a GP and Robert is a farmer.

James Scott, Robert Whitcombe and John Hunter Durran at Swanage, May 1973.

In my new orange anorak, in Arctic Norway 1974.
Photo: P. Bermingham.

Arctic Norway

The British Schools Exploring Society was founded in 1932 by the late Surgeon Commander George Murray Levick RN, a member of Scott's final Antarctic expedition of 1910–13. His aim was to form a 'coterie of pioneers' and the society flourishes to this day. In 1974 it was for boys only and there was a single expedition that year. Our chief leader was George Downie, a tough Aberdonian. We were divided into 'fires'; I was in the geology fire led by John Gunner, an old Wykehamist about ten years older than me, with balding forehead and formidable intellect.

Our base camp was in birch woods, with bilberry undergrowth, beside a fast-flowing stream. Below the valley was a hamlet called Bonnes, about 40km north-east of Narvik. The journey there seemed to last forever but we eventually arrived after a rough ferry-crossing from Tilbury to Gothenburg, a long railway journey via Stockholm and the length of Sweden, with an exciting finale winding down through the mountains from Abisko to Narvik on the Norwegian coast. The final leg was by road in coaches.

Our fire had previously met for a weekend in the Yorkshire Dales and friendships were already forged. We were the first to leave base camp on 24th July, after some filming by a BBC team. We climbed steadily up the valley, taking our boots off for a river crossing in icy cold water. My pack weighed over 50lbs and I was glad of the training on the South Downs Way. The scenery grew more and more impressive, with large snow patches and groups of reindeer. We set up camp in what my diary called a 'pretty fantastic spot' at 900m, beside a partly frozen lake. The clouds lifted to reveal a beautiful evening and I lingered outside the tents after supper, trying to photograph the scene. One of the pictures, of the setting sun behind a BBC tripod, with large patches of snow in the valley below, hangs at home to this day. At the time it was probably the wildest and most inspiring view I had ever seen.

The expedition comprised a reconnaissance phase, a scientific period and a long march. Like the weather, the days were very varied. John Gunner adopted Arthur Ransome's philosophy 'if not duffers wont drown' and gave us terrific freedom to roam the peaks around the Norway/Sweden border in small groups, while undertaking our geological mapping. From the summits at about 1100–1300m we had good views south-east to the giant Lake Torneträsk in Sweden. Some of the mica-schist contained beautifully formed garnets, about the size of small marbles with a perfect dodecahedron shape, which we collected. Interludes at base camp provided an opportunity to relax, read my book *The Lord of the Rings*, play chess and try to evade the mosquitoes.

For our long march, five of us – John Gunner, Patrick Bermingham, Peter

Turner, Craig Young and I – travelled south for three days, crossing the railway line at Bjornfjell, to camp at a lake called Cunojavrre near the Norway/Sweden border. After a rest day and a day helping John who, with a Norwegian geologist, was collecting rocks for radioactive dating, the rest of us set off on our own for three days to climb a peak called Påssosjtjåkka. At 1935m, it lies 19km north of Kebnekaise, Sweden's highest peak.

We made it to the summit, mostly over awkward scree, and were lucky enough to have clear views between the rain showers. Back at our Vango tent, we spent a very stormy night before our return to Cunojavrre. An arduous day's walk was made even more so by a thigh-deep river crossing and a 1200m col in a snowstorm. After another day helping John with rocks, we were given five days to return to base camp by any route of our choice.

The route we chose took us past Losivatnet Lake, descended 400m beside a water chute into Skamdalen and then on to Beisfjord on the Norway coast. Here the steep mountains were beautifully reflected in the still waters of the fjord. On the third day we passed through Narvik, where we bought fresh food such as apples and the following day we camped in Rauddalen. We had time to climb one last peak, with a spot height of 1463m and terrific views of shapely mountains in all directions. On the fifth day we descended to base camp. Pairs of antlers added to our loads made the sacks just as heavy as when we started. On our last night at base camp we were treated to a dazzling display of the northern lights: pale, slightly green, wispy streaks of light flickering across the sky in continually changing patterns.

For me, the BSES expedition was a seminal experience but when I talked to several members on the boat back to England, I was surprised to find that others hadn't enjoyed themselves as much as I had. My diary sums up how I felt:

'Fading already are the memories of heavy packs, wet socks, sore feet, bogs, rain and mosquitoes and left are only the memories of mountains, ridges, glaciers, valleys and cliffs, mountain streams, waterfalls and lakes, the sunsets, rainbows and northern lights, the reindeer and the eagles, the companionship of songs round a campfire; in short a wonderful six weeks.'

View from 'Ice camp' in Arctic Norway, 1974.

Patrick Bermingham crossing Lap bridge at Cunojavrre.

Two

Exeter University

In October 1974 I started my degree course in physical geology at Exeter University, which has a pleasant hillside campus outside the city. The South West of England is an outstanding area for walking, climbing and geology and I soon joined the Climbing Club and the Out Of Doors Society, which organized a programme of walks each term. I was also able to continue the gymnastics which I had enjoyed at Winchester.

The Climbing Club was not particularly encouraging towards beginners. On the second meet of the year, they tackled quite a serious sea-traverse on the limestone cliffs of Torbay. The route passes below unsuspecting tourists in the garden of the Imperial Hotel and includes two 'Tyrolean traverses' where you cross zawns by sliding along a rope. I loved the environment and excitement on the sea cliffs, with the waves just below, but it wasn't to everyone's taste.

The university and city climbing clubs were closely linked and for informal climbing on a Sunday there was a rendezvous outside Boots. A week or two later I jumped into a car heading off for more sea-traversing, this time near Stoke Fleming on the south Devon coast. The leader that day was very encouraging and friendly and it was only on the return journey that I began to realize he was famous. He was Peter Biven, a well-known South West climber who was tragically killed in an accident at the Avon Gorge about a year and a half later.

That November, I joined a weekend trip by minibus to North Wales, where we slept in the straw at Willie's Barn in the Ogwen Valley. It rained! Indeed, my predominant memory of all the university trips to North Wales is of rain, but for me the narrow Crib Goch ridge in wind and rain was very exhilarating. Another student, though – an accomplished VS rock climber – was rigid with fear, with one leg each side of the ridge. It is strange how exposure affects people differently. Only a week or two earlier I had been gripped on a VS climb at Chudleigh, a pleasant limestone crag near Exeter, despite being roped and only a few feet from the ground, but on Crib Goch I had no problem.

The Out Of Doors Society arranged a comprehensive walking programme, with coach trips to Dartmoor, Exmoor, Bodmin Moor and the north and south Devon coasts. It was a great way to get to know the beauty and variety of the scenery in the South West. Some of the walks were quite lengthy and often we fell asleep on the bus back to Exeter. I grew to love Dartmoor, especially around the edges, where the patchwork of fields laps up against the heather and gorse of the moorland. Sometimes, if I had nothing planned at a weekend, I would take the Okehampton bus, get off at Sticklepath and walk up onto the moor above Belstone. Scattered everywhere, the granite tors with their bewildering variety of shapes and sizes add special interest for the climber. All over the moor, there are good easy rock climbs. We often visited Vixen Tor and my favourite spot was Bowerman's Nose. This is a unique granite pinnacle, with a particularly beautiful backdrop, which is climbed by a 30ft V Diff route.

Through the climbing club I met Simon Mumford, who was to become a great friend. Simon stood out at that time, as he was very short (he is the same height as me) and looked very young for his age. Simon was extremely competitive and, although I could easily hold my own at games involving strength after the pub, he was always better at rock climbing.

In the holidays, I continued to visit the mountains with my old friends Philip and Robert. On a December walking tour from youth hostel to youth hostel in the Lake District, we discovered the hard way that there is no easy route from Scafell to Scafell Pike and had the sense to retreat. We also camped in the Brecon Beacons in snow at Easter.

The summer of 1975 saw a return to Arctic Norway with John Gunner and a party from Brathay Exploration Group. It was a much smaller team than the British Schools Exploring Society expedition – just eight members, mostly students. Our base was in the mountains south of the spectacular Skomen Fjord, west of Narvik. My diary notes that the food was much better than the previous year but the mosquitoes and weather were worse. After a rather gruelling three-day walk, three of us climbed Kebnekaise in poor weather. This was our main mountain objective, but the most memorable peak was Lapviktinden, which David Dalton and I climbed in a day from base camp. It has sheer granite precipices on one side, plunging to the Skomen Fjord below, and I found it a most spectacular place.

My first taste of Scotland came in April the following year, in company with John Gunner and a group of his friends. A solo ascent of Marsco rewarded me with the full panorama of the Skye Cuillin. After an exciting traverse of An Teallach, another solo day over Cul Beag and Cul Mor was an eye-opener to the beauty of the far North West, with its isolated Torridonian sandstone peaks surrounded by a myriad of lochans.

Lapviktinden, Arctic Norway 1975.

Bowerman's Nose, Dartmoor. Dave Auger in 1986.

THREE

The Drakensberg

In the summer of 1976, I had the great good fortune to be offered a free, six-week trip to Southern Africa, accompanying my 81 year-old great aunt Veronica, who used to work as a missionary in Zululand. From my childhood, I remembered her as a complete cripple, but after two hip replacements she showed no lameness at all. The invitation was on the condition that I brought a companion and fortunately Philip was keen to come.

From Johannesburg, we spent a few memorable days in the Kruger National Park before travelling to Swaziland and then spending three weeks in Zululand. We even stayed for some time at a nunnery high in the mountains of Lesotho. Although South Africa was a deeply divided country at that time, it was fascinating to visit a new continent and Philip and I found everything colourful and interesting. As a bonus, and well aware of my passion for mountains, Veronica included a week in the Drakensberg.

The Drakensberg mountains run for hundreds of miles in a general north-east/south-west direction, on the eastern side of Southern Africa. They are at their most impressive where they form a massive, 1800m escarpment between Lesotho and West Natal. With their spectacular rock spires, peaks, deep gorges and ravines, it is little wonder that the Zulu word for these mountains means Barrier of Spears.

The upper 1200m of the Drakensberg consists of dark basaltic lava flows and these same rocks, known to geologists as the Stormberg Lavas, also form the mountains of Lesotho. Below the Stormberg Lavas lies the pale-coloured cave sandstone. This rock forms the Little Berg, a grassy plateau itself 600m above most of Natal. The cave sandstone is a soft rock and erosion has formed hundreds of overhangs and caves, famed for their magnificent bushman paintings.

The history of the Drakensberg is a bloody one. At one time the bushmen were the only inhabitants of the region, but early in the eighteenth century Bantu people migrated southwards into Natal and the bushmen were forced back against the escarpment. Before long, successive waves of Bantu tribes fought their way into Natal and the bushmen clung for sanctuary to the most inaccessible caves, resorting to cattle raids in order to make up for the loss of their hunting. The last Drakensberg bushmen died in the early years of the last century, yet practically nothing is known about them apart from their astonishingly beautiful cave paintings made between 200 and 800 years ago.

Between Cathedral Peak and Cathkin Peak, a well-known route called the Contour Path runs for about 50km along the base of the escarpment, above the Little Berg. Cathedral Peak is a prominent peak at the end of a ridge; although it bears little resemblance to a cathedral, next to it stands the unmistakable Bell. Cathkin Peak is also a handsome and dominating mountain, a cornerstone of the escarpment. Philip and I planned to follow the Contour Path and, if possible, climb to the top of the escarpment by the Organ Pipes Pass.

A steep, dry path led us up to the Little Berg from the Forestry Department campsite at Cathkin Peak. Lizards scuttled underfoot and we climbed past protea trees and sandstone overhangs, noting several strange plants and wild flowers. One precaution we had taken, at Philip's insistence, was to bring a snake-bite kit. Since use of the kit involved an intravenous injection, Philip, a medical student, hoped that I would be the one to be bitten! In fact, we only saw one snake but there are a number of venomous species in the Drakensberg. We never saw a single other person the whole length of the Contour Path.

We camped below Cathkin Peak, disconcerted by the faint sound of native drums in the night. Next morning was cloudless and hot. 'My dears, you will freeze in the Drakensberg,' everyone we met in South Africa had told us. It was, after all, their winter and snow can fall at any time of year. Yet we walked in shorts and T-shirts, passing an astonishing mountain called Gatsberg or Ntunja (the eye) which has a huge hole right through it, just below the summit. At lunchtime we were about to leap into an inviting pool in one of the streams when we saw that it was full of freshwater crabs.

On the second night we camped close to a famous cave known as Sebayeni (the kraal) because of its later use as a livestock shelter. This cave alone contains hundreds of paintings but many are sadly faded. On the third day we continued past spectacular peaks called the Pyramid and the Column and camped just before the start of a big thunderstorm.

Fortunately, the following day was cloudless, and we left our tent to climb to the top of Cleft Peak (3222m) by an exposed path graded 'A', the easiest mountaineering grade in South Africa. The exposure was considerable and, in places, the path petered out into sections of scrambling. On the rocks above us, baboons moved around with ease and I was worried in case they dislodged stones on us. We persevered, passing The Camel, a huge camel-like rock at about 2500m, and the unmistakable Organ Pipes at about 2750m. These giant, crumbling basalt pillars not only resemble organ pipes, but are said to produce a similar noise on a windy day.

At the top of the Organ Pipes Pass we stood on the international border, with a fine view of the barren, rocky, flat-topped mountains of Lesotho. But there were still 3km to the summit of Cleft Peak and thunderclouds were gathering. With Philip feeling the altitude and going very slowly, and both of us tired, it seemed a long time before we got there but it was worth the effort. The cleft itself was awe-inspiring, an immense vertical gash of thousands of feet, and we had a stupendous view north along the escarpment to Cathedral Peak and beyond.

Philip Tibbs in the Drakensberg.

Four

Chamonix and Dauphiné

In the summer of 1977, I graduated from Exeter and soon afterwards Simon and I set off, with three other lads, for the Alps. It was my first visit but Simon had been there with the others the previous year. The start was inauspicious: the others were two hours late at the motorway service-station rendezvous, we missed the boat, went to Calais not Boulogne, bivouacked in a hayfield and spent a cramped day driving across France.

We arrived at Chamonix in bright sunlight and found a camping spot in a fir wood below the Argentière téléphérique. The sheer height of the peaks, together with the steep, shining glaciers picked out by the evening sun, put the mountains on a different scale to those of Norway or the Drakensberg and left an indelible impression on me.

The next afternoon Simon and I walked up with heavy rucksacks from Le Tour to the Albert Premier Hut, noting the beautiful flowers and the icefall to our right. Simon had made a bivouac tent from red nylon and we set this up on some rocks a few hundred metres above the hut. According to my diary, 'the evening was fantastic – not cold and incredible views of the glacier and of the peaks between the clouds, including the Aiguille du Chardonnet with its Forbes Arête which we hope to climb'. We crawled into the 'tent' at 9.00pm and I set the alarm for 2.30am.

I needn't have bothered. The condensation from wet nylon made sleeping difficult and it was good to crawl out at 2.30am and see the stars. Walking up the glacier by torchlight was an extraordinary experience, the two of us totally alone, following tracks in the snow. There was just occasionally the distant light of another climber or the unnerving sound of a rockfall. The mist came down and the ground steepened. 'Ici Forbes Arête?' we asked two climbers but they were Spanish and spoke less French than we did.

It gradually lightened and we met parties returning, saying the snow was bad. I suggested we walk up to a col. Simon was feeling the altitude and going extremely slowly, with me tugging impatiently on the rope. Fortunately, the weather improved and we eventually reached the col at the head of the Glacier du Tour at about 8.00am. There was a superb view into Switzerland, the sun lighting the head of the glacier to the left with the black tooth of the Grande Fourche in the foreground. Simon waited at the col while I climbed a few hundred feet up a small peak. I couldn't get enough of the views – but by the time we returned to the valley it was raining heavily.

The weather was to remain mixed and there always seemed to be a reason for one of us to go into Chamonix. One afternoon we took the téléphérique to L'Index, a rock peak in the Aiguilles Rouges, which we climbed. I felt clumsy climbing in boots and with a rucksack but I enjoyed the wonderful views across to Mont Blanc and the Grandes Jorasses. Eventually we decided to drive round to the Dauphiné. We arrived at Col du Lauteret in darkness and pouring rain to find a damp, empty-looking building. The others decided to go on to the South of France for some rock climbing but I wanted to stay in the mountains. There was no animosity, just a difference in objectives, and we unpacked my gear from the car. It took me a long time to get to sleep that night, alone in a damp room with a steady drip from the ceiling.

In the morning I pitched my tent on a good site a few hundred metres above the col. For two days the weather remained very wet, and lying in the tent listening to the rain on the flysheet brought back many memories of Arctic Norway. My book was Jane Eyre and the first paragraph I read went as follows:

'It is a very strange sensation to inexperienced youth to feel itself quite alone in the world, cut adrift from every connexion ... The charm of adventure sweetens that sensation, the glow of pride warms it: but then the throb of fear disturbs it...'

Finally the sun came out and my diary for Monday 1st August starts: 'wonderful, wonderful day'. Leaving the campsite, I passed a shepherd and his flock and followed the path to the Alpe Hut, marvelling at the views of the snowy Meije above the flowery meadows. I tried to climb up to a peak called the Roc Noir but it looked too hard and instead I climbed the Tête de Pradieu (2879m) where some friendly French climbers pointed out the names of the many summits in the superb vista. I descended to a milky blue stream in the valley and followed an easy path beside the river through a gorge and then through cool fir woods all the way down to Le Casset.

The next day I found an easier route up the Roc Noir (3117m) and returned to my tent which, by chance, was pitched so that it got the very last of the evening sun. My diary records 'a wildly beautiful and peaceful evening. Today's summit high above, ambition fulfilled. Only the gentle sound of the flowing stream. A sense of deep satisfaction and appreciation of one's surroundings.'

After one more day alone, the others returned and we drove back to Le Tour. Simon and I walked back up to our bivvy site in the rain, planning to climb the North Spur of the Aiguille du Chardonnet.

This time the night was clear and we walked up the glacier by moonlight. By dawn we were well up the climb. Steep snow gave way to mixed rock and ice. We came across a group of climbers getting in a muddle with ropes and, with the impetuousness of youth and the mantra 'speed is safety', we soloed straight past them all. There was a fine sunrise as we looked across at the seracs on our left, and the climbing was interesting and enjoyable. I led the final pitch to the summit ridge, described in Gaston Rébuffat's book *The Mont Blanc Massif: The 100 Finest Routes* as 'pure, detached and exposed'. From the summit we had glorious views, the descent was fairly straightforward and after a long plod down the glacier we returned, exhausted, to our bivouac site before midday. The North Spur of the Aiguille du Chardonnet is graded *Difficile* and, although my first major route, it remains one of the technically hardest I have done in the Alps.

Next day we drove home.

Simon Mumford in his home-made bivvy tent.

Leading the final ice pitch on the Aiguille du Chardonnet:
'pure, detached and exposed'. *Photo: S. Mumford.*

Simon Mumford on the summit of the Aiguille du Chardonnet.

Five

Libya

The twin-prop F27 plane touched down at a desert strip near Ora, about 150km south of the Gulf of Sirte in Libya. Three of us piled out into a waiting SSL Land Rover and the driver set off across the sand towards our camp, which was about half an hour's drive away. The idea of driving anywhere, unrestricted by roads, was quite a culture shock and I wondered how the driver knew where to go. Within a week I was happily making the same journey on my own.

SSL stands for Seismograph Service Limited, a seismic exploration company with whom I had found employment after leaving Exeter. I started in September 1977, on a salary of £200 a month, and joined an induction course at the company's headquarters at Holwood, a fine country house near Keston in Kent.

At that time, seismic exploration on land consisted of using a sound source, usually vibrator trucks, and laying out a linear array of sensitive recording devices called geophones over several kilometres to record the signals reflected from the different rock layers below. The data, once processed, allows interpretation of the structural geology and is a key tool in oil exploration. Our induction course covered not only geophysics and electronics but practical topics such as first aid and off-road driving.

My first posting was to Port Gentil, a town in the Republic of Gabon on the West African coast. My job title was Assistant Computer and the work involved calculating 'static corrections', an important initial step in processing seismic data. As the junior member of a team of three, I spent most of the time trimming paper records. Many people in SSL would have been jealous of such a comfortable posting in a town with good restaurants, run by French expatriates, and a fine beach. However, I found it rather frustrating that my only experience of the jungle was second-hand accounts from people passing through town to go on leave.

I flew home just before Christmas, via a fog-bound Charles de Gaulle airport in sub-zero temperatures, which was quite a shock after the tropics. New Year found me back in the Northern Corries of the Cairngorms for some ice climbing with Simon's brother Jamie. We camped at Loch Morlich. It was so cold that one morning the tent zip froze shut and we couldn't get out before lighting the primus.

For some weeks I was on standby before being posted to Libya in the spring of 1978. Our camp consisted of three trailers, each with four small, air-conditioned cabins, and a kitchen trailer, arranged in a square around two large tents which were the mess and bar. There were also a few smaller cabins for offices and stores, a shower and, a few hundred metres away, a tented camp for the local labour force, many of whom were immigrant workers from countries such as Mauritania and Chad. The many vehicles included four large vibrator trucks, a water tanker, fuel bowzer, Bedford trucks and about ten Land Rovers.

The twelve expatriates who made up the crew were from a variety of backgrounds and generally friendly. Some of the mechanics had worked in Libya for many years and habitually swore, using the 'F' word in every sentence and sometimes even in the middle of a word. When necessary, they knew how to humiliate cocky young graduates just out of 'f***ing university', particularly those who were reckless with their Land Rovers. I took good care with my vehicle!

We brewed and bottled our own beer, made from bio-malt, yeast and hop-extract. It was very strong. One night someone found me kneeling in the sand outside the mess tent: 'Have you lost something?' All I had lost was my balance. We also had 'flash', pure alcohol, illegally stilled in Tripoli and ordered over the radio as 'special battery acid'. I tended to avoid the flash.

One of my first jobs was to act as cook when our cook failed to return from leave. Having only ever bought meat at a supermarket, it was extremely disconcerting to find half-cow pieces in the freezer. After 'seismic stew' for three nights running, everyone's morale improved when one of the surveyors returned from leave and took over; his father was a butcher and he knew how to cut steaks.

My proper job was to shoot LVLs. LVL stands for low velocity layer, and LVLs were mini-seismic surveys to understand the geophysics of the near-surface layers. I used a dynamite source, generally one kilogram at a time, and a red cable 500m long to which geophones were attached. The recording instrument was in the back of a Land Rover where I would literally melt in the heat, dripping sweat over the precious records.

The desert was very varied: sometimes flat sand, sometimes gravel plain, with isolated dunes or seas of dunes, mesas, buttes and rugged cliffs. Occasionally we found beautiful pieces of fossilized wood lying on the surface of the sand. We managed to drive the Land Rovers to some extraordinarily rough places. Nowadays, health and safety is taken very seriously on seismic crews, with journey management plans, GPS receivers and so on, but in 1978 we just got on with it, driving wherever we wanted, although we were always careful to take water and fuel. If we got stuck in the sand, we let some air out of the tyres and dug the vehicle out.

We worked on a three-months on, one-month off basis. I don't want to make three months working in the desert sound over-romantic. On the whole, I prefer cold places. Sometimes camp would be in the middle of a gravel plain and I found it pretty depressing to wake up and see a huge sun already over the horizon and know that another scorching day lay ahead. Frequently there was trouble with the local labour force and sometimes with the military. But there were times, especially at evening in the sand dunes, when the shadows lengthened and the whole place had a bewitching beauty. I used to wish I could snap my fingers and allow friends to sit beside me in the Land Rover for a few minutes to experience what it was like.

After two tours in Libya, I was posted back to the United Kingdom to work on a crew doing similar vibrator surveys amid the pleasant, green lanes of southern England. We gradually worked across Dorset, Hampshire, the Isle of Wight, Sussex and Kent. Operating large vibrator trucks in populated areas was, of course, very different from the deserts of Libya and I have many amusing anecdotes and memories from this time. I made lasting friendships with two of the crew managers, who were called 'party chiefs'.

In England we worked a five-day week, which gave me the opportunity to catch up with friends at the weekend. One favourite place, where Simon and I often climbed, was Stone Farm Rocks in East Sussex. These sandstone pinnacles have a beautiful setting looking over a reservoir and the unspoilt wooded hills and fields of the Sussex Weald. In those days the climbing was great fun, with good friction and small, sharp-cut pocket holds. Often we soloed, as the rocks are not very high, and Simon, ever competitive, would try to 'burn me off'. Sadly, Stone Farm Rocks has literally been loved to death; these days all the holds are very rounded and the routes are undercut and hard, even to start.

Shooting LVLs.

Driving to work.

A large dune we called the 'big yin'.

Richard Smith on the summit of the 'big yin'.

Vibrator truck in Fernhurst.

Soloing at Stone Farm Rocks. *Photo: S. Mumford.*

Six

Nepal

Nothing I had read or heard prepared me for the first experience of Old Kathmandu when Patrick Bermingham and I wandered through the bazaars on the afternoon of our arrival in December 1978. Kathmandu then was very different from the polluted and tourist-ridden place it is now. My diary recalls:

> 'A seething mass of humanity: beggars, hippies, children, tourists, people of all nationalities; rickshaws and bicycles scattering all and sundry, rings, hoots, smells, joss sticks, drains, carpets, cloths, temples and shrines, narrow streets with wooden balconies either side almost touching above the stalls. An endless tide of people, sound, colour and smell. Tantalizing glimpses of snowy mountains.'

We had joined a British Schools Exploring Society members' trek to Nepal, organized and led by Graham Derrick. Twenty-one of us, with a wide age-range, flew from Heathrow via Moscow and Delhi. The final flight from Delhi to Kathmandu was magical: the whole range of the Himalayas rose abruptly from the plain; ridges and jagged peaks, vividly white, appeared to float above the blue-green foothills below.

The next day we crammed into the back of a local bus to Pokhara, winding our way through the hills on a narrow dirt road. With about thirty people standing and the same number on the roof, it was an uncomfortable but fascinating journey. Much of the land was terraced, with people hard at work. We passed colourful, two-storey houses with overhanging roofs made from local slate.

Our aim was to trek up a series of ridges to the foot of a peak called Lamjung Himal at the east end of the Annapurna range. We walked for about an hour and a half, passing children shouting the greeting *Namaste* and old women carrying unbelievable loads of fodder or wood, before setting up camp in paddy fields. It was Christmas Day and our Sherpas presented a special cake in celebration.

At 6.00 the next morning, after Sherpa tea in bed, we gazed at Lamjung Himal, clear in the cold light and gradually lit by the sun as we had breakfast. We followed the porters through the terracing and tropical vegetation to a ridge in the sunlight, and a magnificent view of the Annapurna range and the sharp-pointed Machapuchare. Then we plunged down 700m to cross the Mardi Khola river by a dramatic suspension bridge. Our Sherpas had a 'brunch' of eggs, beans and chips waiting on the far side. Refuelled, we climbed to a hilltop at about 1200m, where we camped with a great panorama of range after range of foothills, our tents surrounded by hordes of children with smiling brown faces, fascinated by any activity.

The route the following day took us up into the rhododendron forest, a weird place with thick moss coating the ground and trees, and cloud obscuring the views. The porters, amazingly cheerful, sang despite their immense loads. At our campsite, we enjoyed the flowers, including gentians, and glimpses of the peaks, while a pair of large eagles flew overhead. It was a brilliantly starry night and I was glad of my duvet jacket.

Next morning there was frost and a marvellous orange glow in the east, with early sun on the peaks. We followed a procession of baskets through a bright green tunnel of trees and stopped for lunch in a little hollow with sunlight filtering through the wood smoke and a superb view of Manaslu, Peak 29 and Himal Chuli. The nearer we got to Lamjung Himal, the bigger it appeared! We camped at over 3000m and continued up to about 3500m the following day. Our head Sherpa, Tensing, told us about yetis: he had seen one himself about twelve years earlier.

By now it was very cold at night and I was astonished how tough the porters were to manage with just a shared blanket. By the next day, when we reached our base camp at the snowline at 4000m, many of us were feeling the altitude quite badly with headaches. I asked Tensing if he had ever had altitude sickness: 'Oh yes', he said, 'at 23,000ft on Manaslu.'

Unfortunately, despite our hygiene precautions, I had a very bad night with diarrhoea and sickness and missed a trip to a high camp. Once better, I spent some rewarding days on the hills around base camp, walking and scrambling up to 5000m, sometimes alone and sometimes with others but always amid sensational scenery.

On 5th January, as we started our return journey by a different route, we saw a huge avalanche which started high on Annapurna II, the white 'cloud' thundering down a gully for about 2000m, far, far below the snowline. The day after, passing through some attractive villages, my eye was caught by some children's swings, made entirely from wood, with four seats which rotate vertically. Though I sometimes felt embarrassed pointing my camera at everyone, such as an old woman weaving outside her home, the locals were good-natured and got their own back by watching our every move at camp.

Our final full day's trekking was delightful. We camped in a river gorge with some marvellous views but, sadly, next day we reached the road to Pokhara. We pitched our tents by the beautiful lake, watching the mountains turn orange, then pink, and later singing around a campfire with our Sherpas – a good end to one of my best ever holidays.

Swayambhunath Stupa, the Monkey Temple, Kathmandu.

Bridge over the Mardi Khola river.

View to Annapurna II and IV.

Manaslu, Peak 29 and Himal Chuli.

Lamjung Himal.

SEVEN

Gritstone
and Classic Rock

For my birthday in February 1979, I was given a copy of Ken Wilson's *Classic Rock*. This superb coffee-table book has well-written essays by distinguished authors on fifty-five of the best easy climbs in Britain, with excellent photographs and detailed information. Until this time, although I had done some rock climbing at Exeter and with Simon, I was not particularly committed and regarded myself as more of a mountaineer. It's no exaggeration to say that *Classic Rock*, combined with a posting to a seismic crew based in Eccleshall, Staffordshire, kick-started my rock climbing. At the end of the book there is a graded list of the climbs in each area and within a year I had ticked many of the easier routes.

By good fortune I was introduced to John Davis, a mild-mannered, local teacher who was willing to climb, even at short notice, and generally preferred to second while I led. The Staffordshire gritstone outcrops of Hen Cloud and the Roaches, less than an hour's drive away, offered a great collection of routes in the easier V Diff–VS grades. In summer, we climbed in the evenings after work and I loved belaying at the top, on the edge of the moorland, looking out over the Staffordshire countryside in the dusk, before racing down to The Rock pub before closing time.

At weekends, we ranged further afield in the Peak District, climbing on the Eastern Edges and seeking out many more esoteric venues such as Garston Rocks, the Old Man of Mow Cop, Ramshaw Rocks and Kinder Downfall. I liked the texture and even the smell of gritstone and enjoyed the gymnastic style of climbing. With a regular partner and practice, my hand-jamming technique and confidence improved and by the summer I was able to solo two of the *Classic Rock* routes at Birchen Edge and make a runnerless lead of Black Slab at Stanage, which was a much more serious climb before the camming devices called 'Friends' were available.

Outside the Peak District, my first *Classic Rock* route was Sou'Wester Slabs on Arran, with Richard Dowsett, a friend from Exeter. Despite some rain, the climbing was easy but very enjoyable on well-protected granite flakes. The Lake District and North Wales were both less than a two-and-a-half hour drive from Staffordshire and, with John and other friends, I headed straight for the *Classic Rock* routes. Some of the Lake District highlights included Murray's Route on Dow Crag, a superb day on Gimmer and a solo ascent of Napes Needle. In North Wales, the highlight was a glorious day at Idwal.

That summer, Richard and I took my car over to Norway on the ferry and drove to Romsdal. The weather was very poor, with rain almost every day, but we managed an exciting ascent of Romsdalhorn on one of the few fine days. By the end of 1979, I was definitely a keen rock climber as well as a mountaineer.

Early in 1980, I was posted to Australia but, before leaving, I just had time for an excellent week's walking, climbing and skiing in the Cairngorms with Simon and others. It was the conclusion of a memorable year.

Valkyrie at the Roaches.

EIGHT

Australia

The Cooper Basin

Through the mesh window in the door of my canvas tent I could see hundreds of flies, just waiting… I lay on my camp-bed, listening to Grieg's first piano concerto on my small cassette player, thinking wistfully of a recent week's walking, skiing and climbing in the Cairngorms, and postponing battle with the flies for a few minutes. Our camp was amid the sand dunes of the Cooper Basin, in the far north of South Australia, about 50km south of Cooper Creek.

I had been posted to Australia early in 1980. After a few days in Adelaide, kitting out a Toyota Landcruiser for LVL (shallow seismic) work, I had driven up to the camp via the Strzelecki track with Dave Coley, a self-reliant young Australian. It was an interesting two-day drive. We followed the road towards Port Augusta and I saw my first white salt lakes; then we headed north through dry, grassy hills to the Pichi Richi Pass. Between Quorn and Hawker we crossed the Willochra plain, a totally flat area ringed by hills, with a dead straight road for about 40km. We made a short detour up a dirt track at Kenyaka, past some beautiful gum-trees by a creek, to see Death Rock, where the Aborigines used to leave their elderly to die. I was pleased to see my first kangaroos.

Beyond Hawker we passed the Flinders Ranges on our right. These hills were more beautiful than I had expected, with an interplay of sunlight and shade on the gullies and ridges in the evening sun. The tarmac ran out and we stopped for the night at an outback hotel at Parachilna. It was a fine, starry night; the Milky Way looked brighter than in the northern hemisphere and Orion was upside-down.

Next morning we drove on, gradually leaving the Flinders Ranges behind. We passed Lyndhurst, a last outpost of civilization, and continued across flat plains with small, thorny scrub and a few blades of grass, pebbles and dull red sand. A ridge of sand marked the edge of the Cobbler Desert, man-made due to overgrazing, rabbit plague and drought at the end of the nineteenth century. We stopped for lunch at an artesian well; the water was hot and salty and the flies were terrible.

Eventually we reached the Strzelecki Creek and continued up the track, following the dry watercourse, still at a good speed. We were now in parallel dune country. The dunes were a few hundred metres apart and about 7–10m high. With each kilometre it seemed hotter. Finally we came across signs of the oil industry and reached camp by late afternoon.

The camp, at this stage 'fly camp' as the main crew had not yet arrived, consisted of a mess caravan, a small shower caravan, a generator and tents. The seismic lines were bulldozed through the steep dunes of soft, red sand and across the clay pans in between. LVLs involved a technique called 'upholes', which meant drilling a 30m hole and firing charges at different depths. The drillers were a rough lot and we usually had all sorts of difficulties getting their rig and water tanker to the correct locations.

We worked on a three-weeks on, one-week off basis. By now I was Assistant Party Chief and in the middle week of each tour had a lot of managerial responsibilities, what with radio schedules, logistics and administration, including arranging food and fuel for two camps about 200km apart, and frequent trips to the nearest airstrip. I was a lot busier than in Libya or England but, on the whole, the work was enjoyable, especially when the weather got cooler. The flies, unfortunately, remained just as bad. On one or two nights a week we projected films onto the outside of the caravan and sat lost in a different world for a couple of hours.

The grass and trees made the wilderness more interesting than the Libyan desert and there was a lot more wildlife. We often saw kangaroos, dingoes and emus. Hawks and eagles were common and near the creeks we saw galah, pink-coloured cockatoos, and flocks of corellas, white cockatoos. One day we found a huge snake, a scrub python, on the track near camp.

In late April we were hit by a large storm with thunder, lightning and torrential rain. Next morning, camp looked a sorry sight and vehicles became bogged down everywhere. For days afterwards the water remained on the tracks, which have a slight ridge on each side, so that driving was like going along a canal. A few weeks later, though, the desert was carpeted in a fabulous display of wildflowers.

In June we needed to move camp about two days' drive north-east into Queensland, near to a place called Lake Yamma Yamma. I set out with one of our surveyors to reconnoitre the route. As we headed north-east, the dunes disappeared, leaving undulating ground with no bushes or trees. A fence marked the border between South Australia and Queensland and soon afterwards we crossed Cooper Creek at Nappa Merrie. The creek with its pools and stately gum-trees was very beautiful.

Soon afterwards we lost the correct route and followed a track northwards for several kilometres until it ended at an oil rig. Once back on the right track, we still had difficulty as the tracks and the map bore little resemblance to each other. The vastness of the country was very striking. The landscape had the appearance of endless grass plains, although there was always more silica rock than grass. Somewhere ahead there was usually a dark line, marking a tree-lined creek. With only a little less rain, the place would look just like the Libyan desert but it was easy to imagine that a little more rain would make the land green and cultivated.

Quite often there were gates – usually a horizontal bar with tyres hanging below, suspended from a high pole by a diagonal wire – and we saw groups of cattle. For a long while we followed a track beside a fence; here the country was different again, with high, yellow grass and more trees and bushes. Later the track became very rough and we followed the faintest set of wheel marks northward. We stopped at a dry creek just as the sun set. In the distance was a mesa-shaped hill called McGregor's Hill, still 40km south of our destination Lake Yamma Yamma. In no time we had a fire going and brewed tea, followed by barbecued steaks with baked potatoes. It was a memorable night sleeping out beneath the gum-trees and the stars.

Next morning we continued, driving through plains of yellow grass ringed by dark, low-lying hills called The Gibbers, all lit by the low, early-morning sun. It looked like a scene from a Wild West movie and I felt we should have been on horseback. I wondered about the pioneers who gave their names to local features such as McGregor or McKinnon. We came across a much better road which we followed for a time, but later we had lots of trouble with sandy tracks that led to a series of bores, each with windmill and tumbledown shack but no other markings. At one bore we found a group of handsome wild camels. Dromedary camels were imported to Australia from the Indian subcontinent in the second half of the nineteenth century. More often, we came across groups of cattle which would always run along the track in front of us, rather than off to the side.

Finally we reached our destination. Lake Yamma Yamma was flat grassland, stretching away to a simmering blue line on the horizon, with darker hills behind. Three dead cows were a reminder of the hostility of our surroundings. We called in at the local station, Gilpeppe, where the people were friendly and gave us tea but, as we found at other homesteads, they knew nothing of the geography beyond their own land. They must lead very isolated lives.

Our long drive back to camp was relatively uneventful. We carefully plotted all distances and bearings and spent one more night out. A small detour was made to the Dig Tree at Cooper Creek, where there is a memorial to Burke and Wills who perished nearby on their return from the first crossing of the continent. They had arrived back at their depot only nine hours after their companions had given up hope and set off back to the south coast.

The camp move north to Lake Yamma Yamma went smoothly. We drove slowly, in a convoy of about twenty vehicles, and passed the time playing a general knowledge quiz-game called Botticelli over the vehicle radios.

After nine months in the Cooper Basin, we moved on up to Central Queensland for two months, then down to the Hunter Valley in New South Wales, and finally to West Australia where we were based in Busselton, a holiday town on the coast, south of Perth. There, we worked in pleasant Jarrah forests and stayed in a comfortable motel with time for windsurfing before dinner. Paradise, indeed, for a few weeks, after the months amid the heat, flies and sand of the Cooper Basin.

Camp before a storm.

'Uphole' drilling.

Driving after rain.

Crossing Cooper Creek at Nappa Merrie.

Camp move to Lake Yamma Yamma.

Tasmania

I flew to Tasmania on my first leave from the Cooper Basin in April 1980. From the plane I could see most of the island: a wonderful landscape of mountains, forests and lakes. Hobart has a marvellous setting on the River Derwent estuary below Mount Wellington, which rises steeply above the city. I arrived on a beautiful evening and the 18°C temperature seemed very cool compared to Adelaide. I stayed with Hilary and Alan Wallace, who could not have been more welcoming. Hilary is a school friend of my mother and both are doctors living in Taroona, a suburb of Hobart. Their home has great views across the Derwent Estuary.

On my first day I hired a car and drove south-west from Hobart, passing through farmland and then forests of immensely tall gum-trees. From Lake Pedder, I set off up a track through the scrub to Mount Eliza, 1289m. The sun was hot and I had no shorts, so I took off my breeches and climbed in underpants. The whole of the south west of Tasmania is a wilderness area and from the summit I had an extensive view of the remote Arthur Range to the south.

Next day I set off on a longer tour around Tasmania, following the Lyell Highway towards Queenstown. At Lake St Clair, an attractive spot with good views of the impressive Mount Olympus and the pointed Mount Isa, I saw wallabies for the first time. Soon afterwards, the road dropped down Surprise Valley and the distinctive peak of Frenchman's Cap was visible a few miles away, towering head and shoulders above the rest. I climbed Frenchman's Cap with Paul Allum on a much later visit to Tasmania in 1992.

After a night in Queenstown, I followed the Murchison Highway northwards and then drove towards Cradle Mountain, where I booked in at the charming Pencil Pine Lodge. I walked up to Marion's Lookout, with fabulous views of Lake Dove and Crater Lake to each side, and the jagged ridge of Cradle Mountain in front. I noted in my diary that it seemed 'an absolute jewel of a place', although some of the magic was spoiled when it was necessary to help carry a heart-attack victim down the hill later that evening. Next day I drove back to Hobart, mostly on dirt roads, passing the Great Lake.

I was enchanted by the beauty of Tasmania and returned for two more visits that year. In November, I explored the Tasman Peninsular and enjoyed a pleasant walk to Hartz Peak (1255m). At Christmas time, the main objective was to climb Federation Peak (1224m) with the Wallaces' 18 year-old son, Rod. Federation Peak is a spectacular rock summit which has quite a reputation with the Australian bushwalking fraternity. It has a remote location in the south of the island, there is often bad weather, and reaching the summit involves roped climbing. The first ascent was not made until 1949.

From Geeveston, we followed a logging track south-west and set off from the road-head under gloomy, overcast skies. Rod went ahead at a fast pace, answering attempts at conversation with monosyllables or grunts. The 'walking' was very rough, manoeuvring the rucksack between trees, clambering over greasy logs and ploughing through bogs. I had a heavy cold and, to add to the fun, it started to rain.

The path descended to a button-grass plain near Judd's Cavern and morale improved when we caught a glimpse of Federation Peak through a gap in the clouds. We crossed the South Cracroft River and continued, frequently losing the path. Finally, wet and exhausted, we made camp by a river at about 5.00pm after a very hard day's walking.

We woke to a grey morning and spent an awful hour thrashing through 'dead-stick wood' before finding the trail again. The many horizontal branches made progress difficult and the going got even worse as we climbed Moss Ridge, pulling ourselves up steep earth-banks on roots and even pack hauling at one point. My karrimat caught on every tree, provoking much cursing, and it was a relief to reach the Béchervaise Plateau and set up camp. The afternoon brightened and we had good views of the north-east precipices of Federation Peak and the Arthur Range.

When we got up at 5.00am, the sky was clear. As we climbed to the Upper Béchervaise Plateau, with miraculously dry feet, we had dazzling views in the morning sun of the wild scenery in all directions. Route-finding up Federation Peak, following small cairns, was interesting and we only needed the rope for one short pitch. We reached the top at 8.00am and enjoyed magnificent views stretching from the sea in the south to Mount Anne in the north. Even as we filled in the log-book, the sky became overcast in the west. A short way from the summit there was an amazing view straight down to our little yellow tent but by the time we got back there it was raining. Later the sun came out again and we relaxed, enjoying the wild beauty of our campsite. The walk out took a day and a half; at one point we saw a black tiger snake about four foot long.

Federation Peak was a tough trip but a fitting climax to my early visits to Tasmania.

Lake Dove.

Lake Dove and Cradle Mountain.

Rod Wallace on the walk in to Federation Peak.

Rod Wallace and Federation Peak.

PART 2
Peak Years and Alpine Classics

There is much comfort in high hills,
and a great easing of the heart.
We look upon them, and our nature fills
with loftier images from their life apart.
They set our feet on curves of freedom bent
to snap the circles of our discontent.

Mountains are moods, of larger rhythm and line,
moving between the eternal mode and mine.
Moments in thought, of which I too am part,
I lose in them my instant of brief ills.
There is great easing of the heart,
and cumulance of comfort on high hills.

GEOFFREY WINTHROP YOUNG, IN **ON HIGH HILLS**, 1927

Photo opposite: Ski-touring below the Hübschhorn.

NINE

Weekends in Britain

London: Clubs and Weekends

In 1981 I accepted a job as a geophysicist with London and Scottish Marine Oil, later known just as Lasmo. After one last tour in Libya and a first visit to the Pyrenees, camping and walking around Gavarnie and Ordessa with Philip Tibbs, I started at Lasmo's London offices in September. My work involved interpreting seismic data, mostly from the North Sea. In those days interpretation was done by hand. I used coloured crayons to 'pick' the geological horizons, then a ruler to measure the 'two-way time' values and post them on a map, and finally I hand-contoured the values to make maps of the different strata. Given my previous experience in Seismograph Service Limited, I was also responsible for arranging and supervising Lasmo's seismic acquisition. I enjoyed this work the most; it made a break from the rather painstaking seismic interpretation.

Within a few months I had bought a small flat in Highbury Place, Islington, and I joined various clubs, including the London Mountaineering Club. This is an active and very friendly club with a well-maintained hut, Fronwydyr, near Nant Peris in Snowdonia, almost hidden in some holly trees on the left of the track to Elidyr Fawr. The London Mountaineering Club held a monthly slide-show at a central London pub and arranged an active programme of meets, all over the country, roughly every fortnight. I met many characters through the Club and made various friends such as Richard McElligott, Angel Vila and, especially, John Evans. John, from South Wales and about three years older than me, was working for an engineering company in Ealing. His razor-sharp wit enlivened many a Fronwydyr weekend. We were to team up as Alpine partners for several years in the 1980s.

I also joined the Alpine Ski Club and the Eagle Ski Club. The Alpine Ski Club was founded by Sir Arnold Lunn in 1908 and required a proposer and seconder.

I came across the Club by chance when I attended a lecture at the Ski Club of Great Briatin in Eaton Square and went to the wrong room by mistake. I was quickly signed up by the long-standing Honorary Secretary, the Reverend Fred Jenkins. The Alpine Ski Club was not very active at the time but it did hold a splendid black-tie dinner at the Army and Navy Club each winter. Many years later I became the Honorary Secretary myself and, later still, served as President.

The Eagle Ski Club, in contrast, held a very active programme of ski-tours and UK weekend walking and climbing meets. It was to become an important part of my life; many of the friends I made since the early 1980s have been through the Club, including my wife Jay Turner.

After two years in London, I also joined the Alpine Club. It was inspirational and fun to attend monthly slide-shows by world-class mountaineers at their South Audley Street premises. I also made good use of the best mountaineering library in Britain and enjoyed the excellent journal. Though the Alpine Club was not a particularly friendly club at that time, with a slightly stuffy atmosphere, there were notable exceptions, including my proposer David Baldock, George Band, Derek Fordham, Mick Fowler and Ashley and Rosemary Greenwood.

For the next nine years I led a split life. During the week I enjoyed my work at Lasmo but, in truth, I lived for climbing weekends. One benefit of living in London was that we travelled all over the country to climb, including Kent, Dorset, Devon, Cornwall, Pembrokeshire, the Peak District, North Wales, the Lake District and even Scotland. Long motorway drives with late returns to London were normal. I have picked out three unedited extracts from my 1982 diary, to give a flavour of climbing weekends at this time.

Lake District. Monday 3rd January, 1982

'A good New Year's Eve party at John Gunner's with hot wine. Bed at 2.30am, but I kept waking just because I knew I had to get up early. At 8.15am I was waiting for Mark Lowe[1] at the main road, praying he would come as there was a really hard frost, the snow was all frozen and the mist was lifting from the valley.

He came, and we drove up to Langdale as the sun lit up the top of Bowfell just like an Alpine peak. We walked up The Band with lovely views back to snowy Langdale and each corner opening new vistas of Crinkle Crags and Bowfell. Feet crunching in the snow, sun sparkling: it felt good to be alive on such a morning.

Axes out for the climbers' traverse to North Gully. We climbed some steep mixed ground to get into the gully from the right, stopping to put on crampons and climbing gear in quite a steep place (usual mistake). Then up the gully through

---

[1] Mark Lowe was a friend from Exeter. At that time he wasn't a climber but he later became an extremely good mountaineer. We renewed acquaintance at a chance meeting at Stanage and have remained friends ever since.

beautiful frosted rocks. The crux was a small overhang climbed by chimneying, crampons on one wall and rucksack on the other.

So to the top. The Scafells looked big and remote with rather sinister clouds, which just came over Bowfell while we ate lunch but then dispersed again. We had a long plod over to Langdale Pikes in the warm afternoon sun and an excellent day ended with a superb 1500ft bum slide down to the valley, as the sun set, the clouds turned to evening colours and the frost once more gripped the hills.

Next day it rained all day and on Sunday I had to drive through Lake Windermere to get to Ambleside followed by a dreadfully wet drive down the motorway to London.'

North Wales. Monday 26th April, 1982

'On Friday I took the afternoon off and headed for Wales, collecting Paul Clarke[2] from Welwyn Garden City. It was a great feeling to be out of London, heading towards the mountains in summer sun, with the sun roof open for the first time this year, blossom on the fruit trees and dandelions in the grass. We had an incredibly fast drive to Wales: 70 mph all along the A5.

Next morning we woke to glorious sunshine flooding the steep wall of Llanberis Pass opposite Fronwydyr. There was a small patch of snow remaining high on Crib-y-Dysgl. Paul and I drove round to Ogwen and set off up Tennis Shoe Climb. Luckily he led the first pitch and afterwards it was very enjoyable, though sadly in the shade.

We had lunch basking in the sunshine and then climbed up Sub-Cneifion Rib, an enjoyable V Diff, followed by Cneifion Arête, an excellent Alpine-type Mod. At the top we lay in the sunshine before continuing up the Gribin Ridge, over Glyder Fawr and down past the Devil's Kitchen. An excellent day!

On Sunday we climbed in the Llanberis Pass. Nea was the first climb with an awkward step right on the first pitch but the rest of it was good. We nipped down to Llanberis to buy some guidebooks, then back to Crackstone Rib: the first pitch was very exposed and perhaps the most exhilarating lead I have made. We then climbed Wrinkle which was no anticlimax with an exposed top pitch.

It was now about 3.30pm and we drove up to Pen-y-Pass and walked up the Miners' Track to Lyn Llydaw, passing everyman and his dog heading down, and looking at the shady cliffs of Lliwedd. We carried on up to the higher lake of Glaslyn.

---

[2] Paul Clarke was a friend in the LMC. He later moved to Kenya, where he wrote a guidebook on *The Mountains of Kenya*.

I felt very fit and couldn't resist going on up the Y-Gribin Ridge. Paul stayed behind. I stormed up the ridge in fifteen minutes and at the top turned right. It was a long slog up Snowdon but I got there at about 6.00pm.

It was amazing to stand there in shirt-sleeves only, as the sun was going down towards the misty horizon, without having even carried a sweater or anything up there. Llyn Llydaw was a pale blue below, with almost orangey hills stretching away. I promised Paul I would be back at 7.00pm so I couldn't stand and stare for long. I raced on round the horseshoe, running all the downhill sections. It was marvellous to stroll along Crib Goch, reddish rock in the low evening sun, and have it all to oneself, and in late April – not even May. I got back to the car at 7.10pm for the long drive back to London.'

Cornwall. Monday 31st May, 1982

'At the last minute I arranged to go to Cornwall for the holiday with Simon. I picked him up at Reading and we had a beautiful drive down the A303, into the evening sun, England looking at its best with all the fields green. In the morning we continued down to the south west in perfect weather but inevitable bank holiday traffic. On the car radio we listened to the Pope praying for peace while we are in full scale-war in the Falklands!

The Dewerstone was excellent. Sunlit granite in a wonderfully green, wooded valley. Lovely bluebells! We did Colonel's Arête and the Climbers' Club Ordinary which were quite easy, then Needle Arête, and we ended on Central Groove, a superb, steep pitch with perfect holds and protection: possibly the best single pitch I have led. An excellent afternoon's break! We drove on down through lovely Cornish scenery, camping near Land's End late in the evening.

On Sunday, we were at Chair Ladder soon after 9.00am. What a fantastic, granite sea-cliff! We abseiled down. The first pitch of Terrier's Tooth, which I led, was never V Diff – it was desperate! It took all day to do two routes, but routes of superb quality, on perfect rock, in sunlight with the sea below and a profusion of thrift and other wildflowers in every nook and cranny. Especially good was an excellent pitch of about V Diff standard, on super holds, traversing across the crag to reach Pendulum Chimney; and the first pitch of the route proper, the 'V' chimney was also excellent: like so many granite climbs, amazingly steep but excellent holds.

After that we had a much-needed and much-enjoyed cream tea. I had my usual post-climbing headache. Then we went to Land's End itself. It was very pleasant to sit there, contemplating the wonderful sea-cliff scenery, the wheeling gulls, the flowers and the huge swell below. Such a scene as I used to try to imagine in Libya, but the reality was so much better! We ended the day by soloing a V Diff, Land's End Long Climb, just below the hotel. A good route but slightly UJR[3] to solo! So, knackered and battered and ready for a drink or two! But an amazing day's climbing.

Monday was another very warm day. We started at Sennen, where huge waves were crashing against the platform at the bottom of the climbs and occasionally spouting up through blowholes. An atmospheric place! It soon became rather crowded, so having completed the sensational Demo Route we walked through the village to the beautiful sandy bay. I hired a surf board and enjoyed two exhilarating runs into the shore but the water was excruciatingly cold and I couldn't bear it for more than five minutes.

After a pasty and a cup of tea, we followed the twisty coast road round to Bosigran and finished on Commando Ridge, an excellent route which we climbed with a minimum of gear, amid wonderful rock scenery with big waves, flowers, fabulous granite and excellent positions on a knife-edged ridge. It was 7.00pm before we left the Count House for the long drive back to London, stopping at Ivybridge for supper. Bed at 3.00am!'

---

[3] Simon and I between us had developed some private three letter acronyms: 'UJR' stood for 'unjustifiable risk'. Another was 'PMD': 'prudent mountaineering decision'.

Mark Lowe on Bowfell.

Paul Clarke on Gribin Ridge.

Bosigran from Commando Ridge.

The Cairngorms on Skis

On 1st April 1983, I met Michael Vaughan at Aviemore for an Easter with cross-country skis. Mike was an Australian whom I had met through family friends. In Aviemore it was raining slightly and Mike probably thought it was an April Fool's joke when I kept saying there were fine snowy mountains lost in the clouds. We hired skis from Highland Guides and hitched a lift to the Coire Cas car park, arriving in a heavy snow squall. Heading off on a compass-bearing for the Chalamain gap, we found that cross-country skis go quite well over heathery snow. Downhill was less easy with heavy sacks. We established ourselves in the Sinclair Hut, where the concrete floor was wet and condensation covered the roof but the wooden sleeping benches were dry. We decided it was preferable to camping.

In the morning it was brighter, the cliffs either side of the Lairig Ghru were visible and we were able to appreciate the lonely situation of the hut in the wild, snowy valley. We set off up the pass on skis and, despite a faulty binding, I realized how much easier and more pleasant skiing is than walking. By the time we reached the top of the pass, the clouds were breaking up and the sun was coming through, but the wind was increasing, picking up the loose snow. It fairly blew us down the other side, past The Pools of Dee.

We contoured around the hillside and climbed up into Garbh Choire. Cairn Toul and Angel's Peak were visible between gusts of spindrift when we could hardly see anything. We sheltered in the tiny bothy there. It is only about 3m by 2m, made by sacking placed over a metal frame, with stones on the outside. Two friendly Aberdeen climbers were inside and gave us a brew. After a bite to eat we decided to don crampons and climb the Lochan Uaine waterfall. The climb was quite easy and we didn't bother to rope up. Strong gusts of wind were the main hazard. It was strange climbing an open ice-slope. At times the ice was only a few inches thick, with running water underneath. It was quite sunny and the tops were visible. Angel's Ridge looked irresistible – a superb soaring ridge, steepening at the top – and we carried on.

The ridge was long and Mike went quite slowly. The upper section was steeper and rockier but we avoided difficulties by a snow slope to the right. At the top, I made Mike put on his glasses to look at the distant view, but I'm not sure if he saw much. We headed down to the lowest point between Sgor an Lochain Uaine and Cairn Toul and, avoiding the cornice, climbed down a short snow slope to the lochan and on down to the bothy.

We spent only about twenty minutes in the bothy, resting and eating a little more food before leaving at about 3.30pm. The weather had deteriorated badly and the snow was blowing fiercely, even as we attached our skis and fastened shut the bothy door. We crossed the stream and headed down the valley, contouring and gradually losing height, taking care to keep close together. Luckily the wind seemed to be behind us and we lost quite a lot of height but, slowly, I became doubtful that all was well and on getting out the compass we discovered to our horror that we were heading in the wrong direction, directly down the Lairig Ghru.

We turned to face the wind and retrace our route. Immediately I realized we were in for a struggle. The wind was so strong that occasionally it stopped us in our tracks, and all we could do was lean on our sticks and turn our heads out of the snow. More than once I was knocked right over. Our cagoule hoods were fastened so that only the smallest possible opening around the eyes remained; soon large ice crystals formed around this opening. Worst of all, occasionally our skis came off. When this happened it was necessary to remove all the ice around the three metal pins on the binding. To do this, one had to extract a frozen mitt from the frozen ski pole wrist loop and use the tip of the pole.

I had the compass round my neck but if I let go, it blew to the side and I had difficulty finding it with my frozen dachstein mitts. Eventually I held it permanently in my left hand, trailing the left ski pole from the wrist loop. North pointed straight up a steep slope; we were lost and in trouble. It seemed probable that we were heading back into the Garbh Choire. We turned north-east and contoured around the hillside. Much to my relief we gradually turned north and started gaining height. It was a grim struggle onward, with no stopping. Earlier in the morning, in the bothy, we had been discussing our chances of survival if stuck out for a night. Now, it was so cold I had not the faintest doubt we would fail to survive unless we got back to the Sinclair Hut.

At times I could hardly see anything beyond the ends of my skis, but we kept heading north and it was a great relief when we saw one of the Pools of Dee to our right. Now I knew we should get back. It was impossible to judge the angle of the snow: everything was white. But slowly, imperceptibly, we were no longer going uphill. We were on the final downhill run. I was worried that we might miss the Sinclair Hut but we came across first a small post and then the hut, sooner than expected. Relief! A damp hut was the most welcoming of homes. It was almost dark already and I lit candles. Safe in the hut it was hard to analyse just how near a thing it had been.

Next morning, after drying kit in the bright sun, we headed up the Sròn na Lairige ridge on skis and then crampons. The weather began deteriorating fast, so we decided to ski down rather than battle on to the summit of Braeriach. So often, in winter, I have said 'if only I had skis now'. Now, at last, I did. It was marvellous to slide down easily, in perfect silence, and almost an anticlimax to be back at the hut so soon. We skied out next morning and, this time, Mike was able to see the beautiful view of the snow-covered Cairngorms from Aviemore.

The following March I returned to the Cairngorms. Persil had a promotion scheme offering cheap rail tickets, so we all bought a lot of washing powder. We arrived at Aviemore on a perfect morning. There were four of us: John Evans and Paul Krebs, friends from the London Mountaineering Club, and Dave Patterson, a Canadian colleague from work. We all had metal-edged cross-country skis. John and Paul hired theirs from Highland Guides and had mica-soled skis with three-pin bindings. Dave and I both used cable bindings, but Dave had waxable skis and I had the type with fishscale soles.

We used the chairlift to get almost to the top of Cairngorm and continued to the summit on skis, shedding layer after layer of clothing. The descent to the west was tricky, being steep, rocky and icy. (I later saw there was much better snow to the south.) Crossing the plateau to Ben Macdui, the tops of the crags above Loch Avon were the only dark features in a sea of dazzling whiteness and the views from Ben Macdui were magnificent. Apart from distant cumulus above the peaks of Glenshee and Lochnagar, there wasn't a cloud in the sky.

We enjoyed a marvellous ski descent to the south and camped on a patch of flat heather in the Allt Carn a' Mhaim. Paul arrived with the tip hanging off his ski, but Dave dug in his giant pack and produced a spare metal ski tip. Having carried it for eight years without using it in Canada, he saved the day with it in Scotland. As soon as the sun set, the temperature dropped well below freezing but the night was windless and starry.

Next day, we skied on down the valley and made our way on skis and foot round to Glen Dee and the Corrour Bothy. Leaving our camping gear there, we climbed snow slopes behind the hut, using axes for a short, steep section, and then continued on skis to a shoulder near the summit of Cairn Toul. I went on to the summit while the others enjoyed the sun and splendid views. We could clearly see sunlight on the snows of Ben Alder, over thirty miles away. We had another fine ski descent, to the south, going round the Devil's Point, although we had to walk the last two miles back to the hut.

Sleep in the bothy was disturbed by various rustling noises and next morning John found that mice had eaten right through his rucksack to get to the chocolate inside. Again, we emerged to a perfect morning and skied up through the Lairig Ghru on good snow. The scenery was superb, Angel's Ridge and the corries of Braeriach looking particularly fine. From the top we schussed down to the Sinclair Hut in only a few minutes.

In some ways, skiing through the Lairig Ghru, for which the cross-country skis were ideal, was the best part of the trip. We all agreed that for the steeper, icier mountain skiing in Scotland, alpine skis with skins are more suitable. However, the weekend had provided a marvellous ski-tour and we returned to London with faces so brown that people couldn't believe we had only been to Scotland for three days.

Michael Vaughan in the Lairig Ghru.

Dave Patterson, John Evans and Paul Krebs near Cairn Toul.

More Weekends and Chalk Climbs

Throughout the 1980s, between the trips to the Alps and other ranges described in the following chapters, I drove out from London approximately every other weekend to go climbing. When not climbing, I would visit my parents' home at Dell Quay near Chichester, for rest, relaxation and some family tennis. It was rare to spend weekends in London.

Swanage and the Dorset coast was one area I often visited. A favourite route was the Lulworth Cove to Mupe Bay sea-traverse. This splendid adventure has a semi-buoyant traverse, half in the sea, near the end, and I repeated the route several times with different partners. The cliffs at Swanage have many good routes in the easier grades, none better than Benny. This unusual climb has a first pitch entirely of aid climbing, using in-place, threaded slings to traverse horizontally about 15m into the back of a zawn. The route then climbs high up a dark chimney to exit through a small hole at the top onto the outside of the cliff, where a final pitch leads to the top. An equally memorable route was Traverse of the Gods, which I climbed with Richard McElligott.

Another area I visited often was the Brecon Beacons, usually for winter walking. One winter, I was pleased to ski right from the summit of Pen-y-Fan, descending the north-west face and luckily managing not to fall as several walkers were watching. In North Wales, I remember a particularly good weekend climbing on Tryfan and in Llanberis Pass with Bernie Clarke, and another good day with Harry Woodbridge. The highlight, however, was climbing Great Slab and Bow Shaped Slab on Cloggy (Clogwyn du'r Arddu) with Dave Lund, my first route from Ken Wilson's book *Hard Rock*. In the Peak District, highlights included Valkyrie at the Roaches and the eponymous climb at Froggatt.

I celebrated my thirtieth birthday with a fine ice climb in Great Gully on Cader Idris, with Paul Charlsworth. In complete contrast, another highlight at this time was an ascent of Pinnacle Ridge on Sgurr nan Gillean in Skye with Dave Howe, a friend from Seismograph Service Limited, on a scorching hot, August day. In the late 1980s, Ken White, Hugh Murray and I had a series of frustrating failures on the main Skye Ridge, due to poor weather.

An Eagle Ski Club weekend of crevasse-rescue training, based at the Bob Downes Hut in the Peak District in November 1985, was memorable as it was the first time I met Jay Turner who I was to marry many years later. I met Jay again, ski-touring at Chamonix, in a party led by Jeremy Whitehead the following spring and after that we quite often climbed together at weekends, in places such as the Lake District, Dorset, Devon, and Pembrokeshire.

I particularly remember a glorious February weekend, over my birthday in 1987, staying with Jay's friends Denise and Chris Wilson at their cottage in Longsleddale and a weekend at Settle staying with Jay's uncle and aunt, when we climbed at Twistleton on the Saturday and Attermire the following day, walking down the steep path to Settle on a fine summer evening, the air full of tiny flying insects. Jay was very good at bridging and climbing in balance using small holds. On traditional mountain crags, she was much better than me. On gritstone, or strenuous Dartmoor chimneys, she was less at ease and it took me a long time to discover that she didn't like sea cliffs as much as mountain crags.

Fortunately Jay was willing to indulge my passion for sea-cliff climbing. In the late 1980s we found it was much easier to take a short flight from Gatwick to the Channel Islands than to drive all the way to Cornwall, and we had some enjoyable long weekends on the granite cliffs of Jersey and Guernsey. We also visited Lundy and climbed The Devil's Slide, a long desired *Classic Rock* route.

I have always loved sea-traversing and in June 1987 I persuaded my London Mountaineering Club friend Gordon Haines to attempt a traverse from Alum Bay to Freshwater Bay on the Isle of Wight. We took the precaution of letting the coastguard know our intention. It was a hot day and the Solent was very colourful with the 'Round the Island' yacht race. The climb was not entirely satisfactory as many sections involved swimming across impassable caves. The sea was bitterly cold, and quite rough, and near the end I was quite glad that the coastguards were watching us from their rubber dinghy. We were both shivering violently by the time we reached Freshwater Bay. We called the route Albatross but it got no stars for quality.

The next day we attempted a three-star route, Skeleton Ridge, which forms the mainland ridge which descends to the Needles. A 100m abseil gave access at low tide to the beach at Scratchell's Bay, where an initial pitch leads up to the ridge. The chalk is quite solid and we climbed using conventional rock climbing techniques. The third pitch consists of a horizontal knife-edge arête, climbed *à cheval*, with the sea below each side. It was very windy, with the rope blowing out in a great arc. At the end of this pitch, it is necessary to stand up on the arête and layback up a 10ft vertical fin of chalk to reach a large ledge. We both failed to summon up the nerve and backed off!

Back at the Alpine Club, I spoke to Mick Fowler, who had made the first ascent. Mick was already one of the country's leading mountaineers but always friendly and easy to talk to. 'Oh, don't worry,' he said. 'I did the same first time!' With this reassurance, I went back and completed the route, with Bradley Jackson, in 1989. Skeleton Ridge is definitely one of the best multi-pitch climbs within 100 miles of London, with superb situations, and is very easy except for those ten feet.

Aware of my penchant for chalk, in June 1988 Mick kindly invited me on a weekend with some of his friends to climb the Needles, using a rubber dinghy for access. I asked where we would stay. 'Oh, we will just bivvy in a bus stop.' I accepted, with some trepidation, not sure whether bivvying in bus stops was quite my scene. We caught the 7.00am ferry from Lymington as the sun burst through the fog to reveal a brilliant day.

Silliness prevailed as we bought hats and water wings at Colwell Bay before driving to Totland Bay and erecting the boat, which was sturdier than I expected. After some difficulty starting the Seagull engine, we set off for the Needles. From close up they looked impressive. We tackled the middle one first, from a small bay on the south side. Mick leapt up the route and I had some anxiety about my ability to follow. We took turns guarding the boat but, when my turn came to climb, I was pleased to find it wasn't too hard. After grins and handshakes on top, we traversed the narrow arête to the highest point.

I was volunteered to wait on top while the others climbed the outer Needle, for mutual photography. In due course the others appeared, and the requisite photographs were taken. The outer Needle, with the lighthouse, was certainly not a first ascent: there were footholds and nails all the way up. The lighthouse men, after initial reservations, were pleased to show us around; it looked a cramped place to spend twenty-eight days at a time.

We completed the 'triple tick' by soloing the seaward ridge of the inner Needle before landing in Scratchell's Bay to swim and lie in the hot sun. Later we had lots of drinks in the pub in Yarmouth and continued celebrating on my brother Lionel's yacht before bivvying on the beach. Next day, despite some bad hangovers, we managed to climb Arch Rock and Stag Rock, the two stacks at Freshwater Bay.

Bradley Jackson abseiling to Scratchell's Bay.

On Skeleton Ridge. *Photo: B. Jackson.*

On the middle Needle. *Photo: M. Fowler.*

Favourite Climbs

This is a list of the ten British rock climbs that I have most enjoyed. It is, of course, totally subjective and just a bit of fun for readers who are rock climbers.

1	Skeleton Ridge	Isle of Wight	A superb adventure in a unique setting.
2	Benny	Swanage	A most unusual sea cliff climb.
3	Valkyrie	The Roaches, Peak District	Combined with a gritstone day. Is that cheating?
4	Cioch West	Skye	A wonderful mountain V Diff, finishing on the Cioch.
5	Great Slab and Bow Shaped Slab	Clogwyn du'r Arddu, North Wales	Great VS climbing at my upper limit.
6	Terrier's Tooth	Chair Ladder, Cornwall	A fine route on a great crag. A rather unprotected first pitch.
7	Right Angle	Gurnard's Head, Cornwall	Great adventure climbing. Worthy of inclusion in *Classic Rock*.
8	Napes Needle	Lake District	A classic, which I soloed after twice failing in bad weather.
9	Central Groove	Dewerstone, Dartmoor	A superb single pitch route. Bowerman's Nose and Suspension Flake on Hound Tor were also strong candidates but both a little short.
10	Sou'wester Slabs	Arran	Easy climbing in a great mountain setting.

Ski-mountaineering in Scotland

Scotland's mountains, with a good covering of snow, have a unique beauty and wild character which compare favourably with many higher ranges. After my first visits to the Cairngorms, described in an earlier chapter, I returned to Scotland several times during the 1980s, mostly on Eagle Ski Club meets. In that decade there was only one Eagle Ski Club Scottish meet each year and we had astonishing luck with the weather and snow conditions. I always travelled up by the overnight sleeper from London. What a thrill it was to leave Euston on a dull Friday evening and wake up to brilliant snow in the Highlands.

I attended my first Eagle Ski Club Scottish meet, at Dalnaglar Castle near Glenshee, on the occasion of Alan Blackshaw's final Munro in 1984. I remember an amusing incident at Pitlochry station where two senior lady members of the Club were not ready to leave the train; skis and clothing were frantically passed through the sleeper window while a door was held open to prevent the train from leaving. I skied with Hamish Brown, Chris Wright and Sue Baldock, making use of two cars and the Glenshee ski lifts for three half-day tours. In 1985, the Club meet was held at Glen Feshie. For the first of many Scottish adventures, I skied with John Harding and Richard Sykes. Despite quite lean, heathery conditions, we climbed Einich Cairn and Sgor Gaoith.

The 1986 Club meet at Spean Bridge will be remembered by those present for some of the best Scottish skiing ever. On the Saturday, with John Harding and Richard Sykes, I traversed the Grey Corries Ridge, skiing along an elegant, narrow ridge with magnificent views in all directions. I think several of the photographs in the excellent Scottish Mountaineering Club book *Ski-Mountaineering in Scotland* were taken that day. On the following day, joined by David Williams, we traversed Aonach Mor on skis. This was before the ski resort was built. We descended the steep col between Aonach Mor and Aonach Beg and skied down a remote valley back to the Leanachan Forest, clattering down on the frozen surface of a burn long after the snow ran out, racing to be in time for the evening sleeper.

Although the Grey Corries Ridge was possibly my best day ever on skis in Scotland, the traverse of Ben More and Stob Binnein with Ken White the following January, on one of those magical days where the mist lifts and the sun bursts through, was equally memorable. By the time we finally carried our skis up the ice-frosted summit rocks of Ben More, the sun was setting in a brilliant orange sky. We skied down in the gathering darkness, only to have an epic getting lost in the forest. When we finally reached the car, the doors were frozen solid. Having eventually opened a door, we couldn't close it, so we drove off towards Glasgow with the door held shut with a sling. Two days later

I had my first Scottish tour with my future wife Jay Turner, climbing Ben Lomond on skis with lovely shafts of sunlight on the loch and islands below.

The 1987 Club meet was held at Blair Atholl. The splendid baronial dining hall of the Atholl Arms Hotel, with its stags' heads and minstrels' gallery, appealed to the Eagles' style and several subsequent dinner meets were held there, often organized by Jim Harrison and always remembered as much for the convivial social occasion as for the skiing. That year John Harding and I were fit from a Pyrenean trip and, with a willing Richard Sykes, we traversed all three tops of Beinn a'Ghlo from Marble Lodge in another long day.

Bridge of Orchy was the venue for the 1988 Club meet. On the Saturday, with John Harding, Jay Turner and Richard Cooper, we had a superb day traversing three of the Ben Lawers summits and descending into two of the corries. At one point, skiing steeply down to Lochan nan Cat, we all stopped, worried by the steep icy snow with rocks below. We cramponed down about 75m before putting skis back on. Ski-mountaineering in Scotland can be very serious, requiring good judgement, particularly as the weather can change rapidly and the day can fast become a fight for survival in blizzard conditions. But on Ben Lawers the weather remained fine and next day we had a good ski run off Stob Gabhar after some excitement sharing one pair of crampons between two of us, in order to tackle an icy shoulder on the ascent.

In the early 1990s, I missed several years through working overseas, but reading the Club Yearbook it seemed to me that many meets were characterized by poor snow and bad weather. Since moving to Scotland in 2002, there were some years when we never even donned skis. I was beginning to fear that climate change might render Scottish skiing a sport of the past. However, the last few years have seen some excellent snow conditions once again. Eagle Ski Club Scottish meets remain popular and there are now half a dozen each winter.

The Grey Corries Ridge 1986.

On Ben More, January 1987. *Photo: K. White.*

On the north ridge of Carn Aosda. Carn an Tuirc in the background. *Photo: J. Turner.*

My godson Rob Lowe on Sgòr Mòr near Glenshee, December 2010.

TEN

Great Days in
the Alps

Vallée Blanche and Haute Route

The upper stage of the Aiguille du Midi téléphérique rises in a single span from 2317m to 3777m, with dramatic views of the steep north face. When built in 1955, it was the highest cable car in the world and its upper section still has the second longest span. Emerging from a tunnel, at the top of a steep snow arête, there is a glorious view across to the Grandes Jorasses and, in front, a 17km ski run through the most magnificent scenery in Europe, with a vertical descent of 2800m.

My introduction to ski-mountaineering had come when I was in the Cairngorms just before travelling to Australia. I met a couple on ski-mountaineering skis on Cairn Lochan and it was immediately obvious to me that it must be a brilliant combination of the two sports I already enjoyed. I signed up for a two-week ski-mountaineering holiday as soon as I returned from Australia in 1981. The holiday was arranged by the walking company Sherpa Expeditions (as far as I know the first and only time they offered ski-mountaineering) and guided by Alan Jones.

In the first week we were based near Chamonix, in a simple dortoir at Montroc, not quite the luxury chalet some participants were expecting. We learnt how to use our hired equipment, including the adhesive skins attached to the base of the skis for climbing, and ski-crampons, called *harscheisen*, for icy conditions. One day we made an exciting tour in the Aiguille Rouges, crossing the Col des Aiguilles Crochues and the Col de Bérard, with a good ski run down to Le Buet. But for me, the most memorable day was skiing the Vallée Blanche, simply because of the stunning scenery.

After clambering down the narrow snow arête with its flimsy handrail and queues of skiers, the ski route leads below the pale granite slabs of the South Face of the Aiguille du Midi, under the télécabines which cross to Pointe Helbronner on the Italian border and down the Glacier du Géant, with gentle skiing but brilliant views in all directions of peaks such as Mont Blanc du Tacul, the Grand Capucin, the Tour Ronde and the Dent du Géant. Careful skiing is necessary through the seracs and crevasses of the Géant Icefall, followed by an exhilarating schuss down the Mer de Glace, with views of the spectacular spire of the Petit Dru. Finally, from Montenvers, if there is enough snow, it is possible to ski through the woods all the way down to Chamonix.

I have enjoyed the Vallée Blanche several times since that first trip in 1981. In the following year, I skied it with Simon. We set off at the same time as a guided Japanese party, who were all quite elegant skiers. The same could not be said of Simon, whose skiing at that time was simply not up to it. Simon passed the Japanese on each section, completely out of control, before 'cratering' in the snow, much to their amusement.

In 1986, I ascended the Mer de Glace in a party led by Jeremy Whitehead, with the aim of continuing to Mont Blanc. After a whole day of bad weather, stuck in the Requin Hut, we made a serious descent through the crevasses, with two roped skiers in front and the others following exactly in their track; a far cry from the usual schuss. In 1988, with Peter Stokes, who I had met at the Alpine Club, we set out to climb the Gervasutti Couloir but, after one look at the hostile, green water-ice, we skied straight on down the Vallée Blanche and enjoyed it so much we did it again the same afternoon.

My most recent descent was with Ken White in 2006, after a gap of many years. A young French guide took us down a very steep, direct route, teaching us jump turns. Below Montenvers, I was astonished to find the glacier has shrunk so much that there is now a lift installed and, below that, a series of metal ladders just to reach the lift: a dramatic illustration of the effect of climate change within twenty years.

Back to 1981: for the second week of our ski-mountaineering holiday we skied the Haute Route from Chamonix to Zermatt. This famous tour was originally pioneered as a summer route by members of the Alpine Club in the mid-nineteenth century. We set off on an early cable car to the Grands Montets, rising up out of the cloud. An icy descent took us to the Argentière Glacier and a long climb on skins led to the Col du Chardonnet, followed by a scary, side-slipping descent to the Saleina Glacier. Finally, from the Fenêtre de Saleina, we crossed the Plateau du Trient to the Trient Hut with beautiful evening views of the Aiguilles Dorées. My diary that night declares: 'I'm definitely hooked on ski-mountaineering now!'

Next morning we descended the Val d'Arpette to Champex. The proper

Haute Route takes a serious line high on the south side of the Grand Combin, the Plateau du Couloir, but we took the easier Verbier option, staying at the Mont Fort, Prafleuri and Dix Huts. We climbed the Pigne d'Arolla, enjoying great views, and skied down to the Vignettes Hut which has a spectacular position on top of a cliff. On the last day the route crosses three cols to reach Zermatt. On the long, final climb up to the Col de Valpelline, I went ahead at my own pace. I knew that the Matterhorn should come into view and eventually the unmistakable summit triangle appeared above the snow. We had a great ski down the Zmutt Glacier towards Zermatt. Looking at all the 4000m peaks surrounding Zermatt, with long and, as yet unfamiliar, names such as Ober Gabelhorn and Zinal Rothorn, was an eye-opening moment: I realized that there was more to the Alps than just Chamonix. I would return to the peaks around Zermatt again and again in the next ten years.

View from the Aiguille du Midi to the Grandes Jorasses.

The Aiguille du Midi téléphérique.

Near the Col du Chardonnet.

The Plateau du Trient with the Aguilles Dorées and the Aiguille du Chardonnet in the distance.

The Gervasutti Couloir: we took one look and skied on down the Vallée Blanche.

Descending the Zmutt Glacier, Dent d'Hérens in the background.

SWITZERLAND

Bern ■

Thun ●

Grindelwald ●

Jungfrau ▲

Finsteraarhorn ▲

BERNESE OBERLAND

Lausanne ●

Weisshorn ▲

Dente Blanche ▲

Visp ●

Geneva ■

Arolla ●

Zermatt ●

PENNINE ALPS

Argentière ●

Matterhorn ▲

▲ *Monte Rosa*

Chamonix ●

Mont Blanc ▲

Aosta ●

Cogne ●

GRAN PARADISO

Gran Paradiso ▲

FRANCE

VANOISE

Grenoble ■

Turin ■

Barre des Écrins ▲

Briançon ●

ÉCRINS

● Gap

AUSTRIA

BERNINA
ALPS *Piz Bernina*

ORTLER
ALPS

Bolzano

Bormio

Disgrazia

Presanella

Adamello BRENTA
DOLOMITES

Sondrio

Trento

Como Lecco

Milan

ITALY

Verona

The
European
Alps

Bernese Oberland

In 1982, two of us teamed up for what turned out to be a memorable summer season in the Bernese Oberland. My companion was Alan Winton, who I had met in Edinburgh while soloing on Salisbury Crags a few months previously. Alan was a first year student at Edinburgh University, aged only 17. He had never before travelled beyond Scotland, let alone overseas. I was therefore the only one with Alpine experience and had all the fun of planning the holiday, but Alan was extremely fit and enthusiastic and so an ideal companion.

We travelled to Switzerland by rail, still the most romantic way to travel to the Alps, even in the 1980s. We each had two large rucksacks, one filled with climbing gear and the other with camping gear, and these took up an antisocial amount of space in the rather cramped six-man couchette. The total cost of our two weeks' holiday was about £250 each.

We started by camping at Grindelwald. From the door of the tent, we had a fine view of the Wetterhorn and this immediately became our first objective. For the first two days we walked in the valley during bad weather but I slowly realized that the poor weather at Grindelwald was very local, so on the third day we went up to the Gleckstein Hut. I remember this as a very friendly place. Outside there were several tame ibex and some clown managed to tempt one of the creatures all the way into the common room by laying a trail of salt on the floor!

In the morning we woke up to thick 'Scottish' mist. No other parties left the hut, but as Alan had never been on a glacier, we decided to go at least that far. We walked up a moraine path for about an hour and gradually the mist thinned and we started to glimpse the moon. It turned out to be one of those magical days, with just the highest peaks emerging from a sea of cloud below. We had the entire mountain to ourselves. I remember arriving on the Wetterhorn summit completely unexpectedly, just as Alfred Wills did on the first ascent. We descended back into cloud and it rained the whole way down to Grindelwald.

Two days later we caught the train to the Jungfraujoch and climbed the ordinary route up the Jungfrau. At the top we met an unhappy guide who was cursing that his client was so slow. We paid for our late start by finding very soft snow on the glacier as we plodded across to the Mönchjoch Hut.

Next day we climbed the Gross Fiescherhorn by the north-west ridge – quite a short expedition but a very enjoyable route up a beautiful snow arête. After a day hut-bound in thick mist, we climbed the Mönch by the north-east ridge, another very pleasing snow ridge with extensive views down to Grindelwald and the grassy hills beyond. We descended the south ridge and continued down the Jungfraufirn to the Koncordia Hut. Owing to the recession of the glaciers, the hut is reached up a long series of ladders. I was intrigued to find a chair there donated by the Eagle Ski Club.

Making a very early start the following morning, we slipped quietly out of the hut at 2.00am, and climbed the Hasler Rib on the Aletschorn, returning by the same route. Such an early start wasn't necessary as we were back in the hut soon after midday. We plodded back up the Jungfraufirn the next day and took the train back to Grindelwald.

Our final fling was an ascent of the Schreckhorn by the south-west ridge. The six-hour walk from Grindelwald to the Schreckhorn Hut must be one of the finest hut walks in the Alps. We took it leisurely and enjoyed the flowery lower slopes of the mountain. The ridge provided a splendid rock climb which I thoroughly enjoyed once the chilly early morning wind had died down.

Having climbed five 4000m peaks and the Wetterhorn in less than a fortnight, I returned home far too conceited. Luckily this didn't last long: a few weeks later a friend and I set out to climb Bowfell Buttress in the Lake District and got so completely, utterly lost that we couldn't even find the mountain.

This account is based on an article published in the Alpine Journal Vol 99 entitled 'Innocents Abroad: An Alpine Season in the Eighties'. It was modelled on an article written by Charles Warren: 'Innocents Abroad: An Alpine Season in the Thirties', in the Alpine Journal Vol 97; and aimed to show that little changes apart from the cost.

Ibex outside the Gleckstein Hut.

Alan Winton on the Wetterhorn summit.

The Finsteraarhorn from the Schreckhorn.

Pennine Alps: Winter and Summer

As we climbed on skins towards the Cabane d'Ar Pitetta above Zinal, the weather deteriorated and it started snowing. I'd forgotten the effort involved, the weight of the pack, the slow pace, the slightly sore heels and aching shoulders. Thunder rumbled overhead, the snow poured down harder than ever and Anne's hair was completely matted with ice. It seemed impossible to believe that only the previous day we had been driving across France in warm spring sunshine. Finally we staggered up to the hut at 2786m and spent the best part of fifteen minutes hacking away at the ice to get the door open.

This was my first Eagle Ski Club tour, in May 1983. The other participants were David and Sue Baldock, Justin Blake-James, Anne Twedell, Ian Purslow, and Giles Dessain, and the tour was guided by the well known Swiss guide Denis Bertholet. Zinal lies at the head of the steep-sided Val d'Anniviers. The plan during the first week was to traverse east to the Mattertal valley, spending two nights at each of three huts. The peaks between the two valleys form the French-German divide in the Valais and are dominated by the Weisshorn, one of the most beautiful mountains of the Alps.

The hut soon looked more homely and part of the evening was spent hanging in various harness combinations from the beams. It was a cold place to stay, though, with only one blanket apiece. In the morning, with light sacks, we skinned steadily through soft powder snow towards the foot of the Younggrat Ridge on the Weisshorn. We had superb views of the Schalihorn and Zinal Rothorn and, as we gained height, the impressive Dent Blanche. We used *harscheisen* once the going became steeper and more crevassed and halted in the sun on a small top at 3575m, with good views to the distant Mont Blanc range.

The ski down was superb, on perfect powder snow, and even I was able to make a perfect 'S' shaped track, of which I was very proud. In the afternoon we had an autophon (avalanche transceiver) practice. I felt my own test was a little unfair as Denis had thrown the 'body' well beyond the 'avalanche area' into soft snow.

Next day we crossed the Col de Milon and climbed to the Tracuit Hut and the following day we attempted the Bishorn in rather windy conditions. I started to get a terrible altitude headache and could do little but slump down when we reached the small col between the two summits. The weather forced a retreat anyway. One member was having trouble skiing, falling a lot and Denis was yelling at him in French and English. It was a case of survival skiing, with stem turns, wind and snow blasting in one's face and the uphill track completely obscured. Denis' navigation was faultless and back at the hut I lay down for half an hour to recover from my headache.

In the morning we descended steeply beside the Turtmanngletscher and skied up the Bruneggletscher. Amazingly, the clouds all broke up, the sun came out and we continued on ski and foot to the summit of the Brunegghorn, where we had a great view of the Weisshorn and all the Zermatt peaks. After a good ski down we spent the night at the very pleasant, beautifully sited Turtmann Hut, admiring the views of the Bishorn.

We completed the first part of our tour by climbing the Barrhorn, descending a wide, steep gully between large rock walls to return to the hut and, the following day, taking a complex route north-eastwards to reach the Jungtal Valley. It was strange to see trees again, and spring crocuses, and admire the attractive stone-roofed chalets. From Jungu we caught a small télécabine down a long slope to St Niklaus.

In the second part of our tour, we skied from the small hamlet of Gspon up the Wyssgrat ridge, with great views of the Mischabel Peaks, and finished a long day at the Simplon Hospice, a huge, four-storey building, originally built as a barracks for troops in Napoleon's time. It was run by a handful of monks providing simple accommodation for travellers.

Unfortunately, the weather restricted us to short day tours for the remainder of the trip. However, the holiday had rekindled my enthusiasm for ski-mountaineering and been an eye-opener to the opportunities in the Pennine Alps. I resolved to return as soon as possible, with the Zinal Rothorn and Weisshorn on the hit-list.

I was back in August! I met up with LMC member and school teacher Steve Rydon, at Sierre. From Zinal, it was a long walk up to the Mountet Hut and Steve, who had already had a week in the Alps, left me well behind on the long moraine trail. We reached the hut in a hailstorm.

Surprisingly, the morning was clear, with a starry sky beginning to lighten and a good view of the Dent Blanche. We climbed beautiful granite-gneiss to the summit of Besso, with amazing views of the Weisshorn, Matterhorn and Dent Blanche, and distant views of Mont Blanc and the Oberland peaks. After awkward down-climbing, we traversed Blanc de Moming and made a long descent to the hut. I had my normal first-day headache but, after supper, I recovered and felt a profound sense of well-being, sitting outside the hut looking at the fine view of the North Face of the Ober Gabelhorn.

Next day we climbed the Pointe de Zinal, with more great views, and the following morning we left the hut at 2.30am, under brilliant stars and the odd meteor, heading for the North Ridge of the Zinal Rothorn. Headtorches were essential for the long plod up the moraine path and then up glacier slopes. Near dawn we reached the steep snow arête which swept up in a magnificent, exposed position to the Epaule du Rothorn. We could see the North Ridge rising in a series of spectacular gendarmes just catching the sun. Cloud was sweeping around and we saw Brocken spectres on the mist to the west.

The ridge was formed of marvellous granite-gneiss. At first the scrambling was quite easy, then there were some spectacular gendarmes, with one particularly exposed one, the Rasoir, and finally the last tower, climbed at about Diff standard on perfect holds. Moving together, threading the rope round flakes and belaying occasionally was lengthy and thirsty work but we reached the top at 10.15am.

The descent went surprisingly smoothly. We abseiled the steep tower and I got told off by a guide for letting out too much rope while moving together. Finally we climbed back down the snow arête in oven-like heat, with bright sun but mist and clouds. We got back to the hut at 4.00pm, just before afternoon rain, after a splendid mountain day.

It was gently raining in the morning and we made a leisurely descent to the valley, enjoying the grass and the flowers. Unimpressed by the campsite at Zinal, we booked into a hotel and enjoyed the luxury of a hot shower, followed by a good meal and a excellent night's sleep.

We woke to a fine view of the cloud lifting off Besso and, after fresh rolls for breakfast, we sorted our kit in the hot sun. We then drove down the valley, having a picnic lunch in a picturesque spot above Grimentz, and on up to the dam at Moiry. An hour's steep walk, at high speed, led to the Moiry Hut. The following day, on the North Ridge of the Grand Cornier, was perhaps the most enjoyable of the holiday. Snow climbing was followed by superb rock to a wonderful summit with, surely, one of the most spectacular views in the Alps.

For the second week we were joined by Michael Vaughan. We drove up the very scenic Turtmann Valley, past fir trees and fine waterfalls, 'bewildered by the incredible beauty', according to my diary. We walked up to the Turtmann Hut in hot sunshine. The hut was every bit as lovely as I remembered it from May, and we enjoyed a fine evening watching the sunlight on the Bishorn long after it had left the hut.

It was a fine, starry morning when we woke at 4.00am and followed the moraine path, watching yellow morning light creep down the face of the Bishorn. Due to a fortunate route-finding error, we missed the turn-off to the glacier and reached the shaly Schöllihorn with an incredible morning view of the sun and distant mountains above a cloud-filled Mattertal valley.

We continued to the Brunegghorn. The others were going very slowly and I decided to solo the north face, which is 400m high at an angle of 57 degrees. It felt immensely exposed out on the face and I learnt several lessons, such as the need for stiffer boots, helmet, braces and a partner! I arrived right at the summit and waited a long time for the others who climbed the north-east ridge.

Next day we climbed the east ridge of the Bishorn, which was quite straightforward despite an 'AD' grade. In my diary, I complained about my companions: 'Steve is very slow and not fully competent on snow and ice, Mike has to learn how to handle the rope and move faster on rock. Me – I'm just impatient!' The following day we made an exciting traverse of a peak called Les Diablons, which was not in our guidebook, to return to the car. We drove down the valley, stopping for hot chocolates and then beers, and continued round to the campsite at Randa in the Zermatt valley.

The sun hits the Randa campsite late in the morning and breakfast ran into lunch. Eventually I got impatient to leave and we set off for the Weisshorn Hut. Initially the path was relentlessly steep, the buildings at Randa looking smaller and smaller below. The hut warden was grumpy but the views were great, as with all Swiss huts.

Next day got off to a bad start with some quarrelling, but things improved once we reached the east ridge. There was some excellent scrambling, never more than Diff in standard, over several gendarmes on superb rock, followed by an interesting snow climb past various crevasses with icicles sparkling in the sun. Finally we made it to the summit, the fifth highest in the Alps, and well-earned views of all the peaks we had climbed.

The Weisshorn was a fitting climax to the holiday. More than ever, this trip confirmed to me that the Swiss Alps were my favourite mountains and nothing could better a climbing holiday amid their variety and beauty. As always, back at home, I waited anxiously for my slides. They did not disappoint. Two enlargements hang in our living room to this day.

Fresh tracks in the snow.

The Ober Gabelhorn from the Mountet Hut.

Early morning view from the Brunegghorn.

Steve Rydon on the east ridge of the Bishorn.

Steve Rydon on the Grand Cornier.

A Night Out on the Matterhorn

In 1985, I had a memorable summer season. This time I had a single, extremely competent partner, John Evans. John was a much better rock climber than me, super fit and exceptionally well organized. I never remember waiting for John or seeing him faff with his kit. On 17th August, I left home at 4.10am, collected John from Acton at 5.00am and we reached the campsite at Randa at 11.00pm after a long day's driving.

We rose late next morning, once the sun hit the tent, and had breakfast in 'the garden' with fine views of the mountains and a clear blue sky. I hadn't yet learnt that I need time to acclimatize in the Alps, so our plan was to start by traversing the Ober Gabelhorn. Unfortunately, the Rothorn Hut is a five-hour walk, so we couldn't spend too long enjoying the pleasant Randa campsite. My pack felt appallingly heavy as we walked up the Trift Gorge above Zermatt. Mica crystals glistened in the sun as we ground up moraines to the hut. John powered ahead, but I still got there in an hour less than Collomb's guidebook time. I was already feeling the altitude slightly.

After a poor night's sleep, we left at 4.30am, putting on the rope straight away, and were soon climbing the glacier. We made our way to a snow shoulder and then up rocks to reach the Wellenkuppe summit at 6.00am. There was a cold wind but a fine view of the Ober Gabelhorn ahead, although the Matterhorn and the Zinal Rothorn both had strange cloud caps.

A little farther on we reached the Grand Gendarme. This was quite hard, with strenuous pulling on thick, icy, fixed ropes, and very cold in the wind. We continued up to the Ober Gabelhorn in a fine position, with the north-east face on our right. There were some tricky bits of rock climbing near the top and we reached the summit at 10.00am.

Pausing only for some photographs, we headed straight down the Arbengrat. What a long ridge! We started moving together but soon made some lengthy abseils. On and on the ridge went, never easy, with awkward moving, one at a time, hands in gloves on good holds. Looking back up at tower upon tower of reddish rock was very impressive. I was suffering from the altitude now and feeling very tired.

At the bottom, Mont Durand looked far longer and steeper than I had expected. By now I was feeling dreadful, dehydrated and nauseous. I went in front, at a snail's pace and, skirting around the summit, we made our way to the Col Durand at 4.00pm. The Schönbiel Hut looked a very long way down. We had been on the move for more than twelve hours, hardly stopping or eating. When we finally got to the hut, I felt too ill to eat supper. The next day was declared a rest day, before tackling the Zmutt Ridge on the Matterhorn.

I am never able to sleep before a big climb and woke John five minutes before our alarm was due to go off at 2.00am. I forced down as much coffee and liquid as possible and even managed one slice of bread and jam. We left at 2.30am, descending the zigzag path, which seemed much longer by torchlight, and clambering steeply down to the Zmutt Glacier. It was a superb night; there was not a sound except for the occasional movement of rock on the glacier and our own footsteps, just a slight wind on our faces and the odd shooting star in the sky.

Little mounds on the glacier seem so different in the dark. We plodded steadily across until we had to stop and put on crampons for a troublesome crevasse at the foot of a steep side glacier. It was a very long climb to the snow arête on the Zmutt Ridge, almost 1000m, with tricky route-finding in the dark, snow climbing, rock climbing and endless scree. It was 8.00am when we finally reached the arête, in a superb situation with the glacier below the north face on our left.

The half-hour climbing the arête was enjoyable. Near the top we saw three military jets approaching and climbing vertically into the air in front of the north face. Beyond the arête, we took off crampons to traverse some pinnacles and then followed a fine rock ridge slanting up the right, moving one at a time at first, and together later. To our left was the enormous overhang of the Zmutt Nose, with the Zermatt valley down below and the familiar profile of the Täschhorn-Dom ridge in the background.

The ridge led up into the blazing sun. It was early afternoon and we had been going steadily since 2.30am. I was so dehydrated that I found it hard to swallow. The route went out onto the west face and John led a difficult pitch where we used a piton for the belay. Beyond this, route-finding became difficult; the whole face was composed of very loose, slabby, red rock and finding even semi-secure belays was very hard. At one point, a party on the Italian Ridge precipitated a huge stone fall down the face to our right.

An Italian guide with two clients now overtook us, and kindly left their rope for another very difficult pitch over loose, wet and verglassed rock. A pitch or so later we found a dribble of water and spent a long time filling my water bottle, which was well worthwhile. By now, the view was incredible; we could see all the peaks of the Mont Blanc massif and range after range of peaks to the south. We now had the additional danger of stone fall from the party above, which had us cringing to the rock once or twice. Often the peace was disturbed by helicopters buzzing around the mountain.

After another three rope-lengths, we at last regained the Zmutt Ridge and the shining roof of the Schönbiel Hut looked astonishingly far below. The rock was much better on the ridge, but we continued to move one at a time. Eventually we reached the Italian summit at 5.30pm. We had it entirely to ourselves and the view was wonderful. We couldn't have asked for better weather; there wasn't a cloud to be seen.

Time for a precious mouthful of water, a few dried apricots and another headache pill. I even lay down and closed my eyes for two minutes. Then we carefully moved on to the Swiss summit about 300m away and started down the Hörnli Ridge. At first it was much easier ground, but quite snowy, and we had to stop to put on crampons. The ground steepened and a series of fixed ropes appeared. We made several abseils from fixed metal stakes, losing height quite quickly, and continued down a sort of path in places, stopping to remove crampons. Then, after the shoulder, the ground steepened again and we resumed moving one at a time.

We felt the Solvay Hut must be quite close but there was no sign of it and suddenly – very suddenly – in the space of a few rope-lengths, the light went completely. All that was left was a dying glow in the west; we couldn't see where the route went and it was too dark to see the holds. We found a reasonable ledge, just below the ridge, and settled down for the night. I dug around in my pack, sorting things out, finding my torch and so on, and turned round to see John already completely prepared in his duvet, cagoule, and balaclava. We both stayed tied on, and squeezed our lower halves into my orange bivvy bag. Supper was a few mouthfuls of water, three biscuits and two dried apricots each. A look at the watch, and to my surprise it was already 10.00pm.

The stars shone with wonderful brilliance and soon it became very cold. We were both tired and there was little talk. The first time I looked at my watch it was already after midnight and a bright planet had gone behind the ridge. The next watch check was best: it was now 3.15am. It was strange to think that twenty-four hours earlier we were crossing the Zmutt Glacier. The point of contact between my bum and the ground was getting very painful and I started checking the watch more and more often but there was no sign of dawn. And then, at about 5.15am, quite quickly, an orange glow spread behind the mountains to the north-east.

I got out of the bivvy bag and stomped around on the ledge but it was too cold to start moving. Breakfast was one biscuit and a sugar lump each. We left at about 6.30am, just as the sun appeared over the shoulder of the Rimpfischhorn. We quickly warmed up and soon met the first guide and clients coming up; before long we passed an endless stream of ascending climbers. We reached the Solvay Hut after a tricky piece of down-climbing which I was glad we hadn't tried in the dark. Below there was more technical climbing and then a lot of moving down semi-paths between rocks, with little awkward bits in between. The whole face was covered in dust, but at least the ascending parties made the route obvious.

The hut steadily drew closer but there were still some steep sections, with a huge drop down the east face on our right, before we could finally unrope. We got to the Hörnli Hotel at 10.00am. Our Italian friends were outside, having made it down by torchlight the previous night. We each consumed a litre of *Apfelsaft* with no trouble, and enjoyed an excellent ham omelette. Somewhat reluctantly, we left at 11.00am, John heading down to Zermatt and I heading back down to the Schönbiel Hut to collect a few items, such as an ice hammer, which I had left to lighten my sack.

The three-and-a-half-hour walk down from the hut to Zermatt was agony on my feet. The sky clouded over, it started to rain, and the time on each signpost was watched critically. I would have taken a taxi through the town but there were none. Back at the campsite we were reunited. John also had very swollen feet. After a good shower, we had a fine celebration meal and, back at the tent, I fell asleep before even having time to get into my sleeping bag.

We spent a pleasant rest day at Randa and then drove to the Grimsel Pass, where we found dormitory accommodation and had two more rest days, enforced by the weather, but probably needed. We then climbed up to the Oberaarjoch Hut, still in poor weather. The hut was approached by a ladder and fixed chains. To our surprise there was no warden. Luckily a party of friendly Austrians appeared and shared their rations.

Next day was fine, with snow-covered peaks and good light. Breaking trail across the glaciers towards the Finsteraarhorn Hut, we several times went waist-deep into crevasses. At the hut, we enjoyed a good lunch and a fine view of the Gross Grünhorn, and bought wine to repay the Austrians for feeding us the previous night.

We were really fit by now, and were the first up the Finsteraahorn, kicking steps all the way up the glaciers to the Hugisattel. We mostly moved together up the final ridge, keeping out of the cold east wind where possible. There was interesting mixed ground, longer than expected, but we reached the summit by mid-morning. It was another superb viewpoint. A balloon approached rapidly from the direction of the Schreckhorn and passed overhead with little room to spare.

We clambered quickly but safely back down the ridge, passing our Austrian friends, then a Dutch party and finally, on the glacier, an elderly German couple who insisted on shaking our hands and thanking us profusely for the steps. The snow was already soft and balling up dangerously by the time we returned to the hut at 2.15pm and I was glad we were no later. The other parties all returned, eventually, and rather too much *Graveline Dole* was drunk in celebration.

Setting out for the Gross Grünhorn the next morning, we chose to climb the south-east ridge of the Grünegghorn en route. This was a mistake, as it was much longer and more serious than we had expected. By the time we reached the Grünegghorn summit, we decided to leave the Gross Grünhorn for another time. On the following day we walked back out to the car at Grimsel, and drove off down the valley, finally camping by the beautiful lake at Lungern with its green, wooded hillsides and cuckoo-clock chalets. This time we took two days to drive home across France.

The Matterhorn from the Wellenkuppe.

The Ober Gabelhorn, north-east face.

John Evans descending the Arbengrat on the Ober Gabelhorn.

The Wannenhorn in early morning light.

A balloon over the Schreckhorn and Lauteraarhorn.

The Finsteraarhorn, from the east.

John Evans on the Grünegghorn.

Bernina and Monte Disgrazia

In August 1988, I returned to the Alps with John Evans, after two summers away. We chose to start in the Bernina Alps, an area new to both of us, and drove out via Germany, spending a night in the Black Forest. Reaching Pontresina the following afternoon, we took a horse-drawn carriage up the beautiful, forested, lower reaches of Val Roseg. This seemed a good idea to me, as it was clearly a lot quicker than walking, but I noticed John making surreptitious attempts to hide his rucksack as we passed descending climbers. I managed to keep up with him on the walk to the Tschierva Hut and we arrived just in time for the evening meal. The dormitory was crowded and a German snored loudly in my ear: a far cry from the lonely wilds of Arctic Norway or the Karakoram.

Our first peak was Piz Roseg. The initial pitch above the glacier, which I led, was one of my most frightening moments in the Alps. I had cold hands on poor holds, plastic boots, also on poor holds, no helmet and a nasty bergschrund lurking below. It was definitely a place for staying calm. Easier, pleasant granite rocks led to the upper snowfields and we cramponed steadily up to the top. Unfortunately, the south-east summit, separated by a deep gap, was higher, so we spent an hour going out and back with some awkward rock scrambling. We descended the rocks back to the glacier with a series of abseils and passed some very large crevasses on the return to the hut. A 3937m peak and an eleven-hour day were a bit much for the first day out and I didn't feel I fully enjoyed the climb.

Next morning, up at 3.00am to starry skies, we set out for the famous Biancograt on Piz Bernina. A series of moraine paths led up to a glacier at first light and, above, four pitches of sustained front-pointing on very hard ice led to the Fuorcla Prievlusa. Somewhat daunted by the seriousness of the approach, we reached the col at 7.30am. An hour and a half of scrambling along a rock ridge led to the foot of the Biancograt. It was time for sunglasses.

The ridge curved upwards with sun on one side and shadow on the other, looking very beautiful. There was no one else in sight. Underfoot, it was very icy, requiring careful crampon work, but the situation was superb. I think that John's photograph, on the cover of this book, portrays it well. I felt quite thirsty and went slowly but we reached the top of Piz Alv at 11.45am. The view on up to the summit of Piz Bernina looked rather daunting, with a large rock tower, but the climbing was good and easier than I expected. It was nice to relax on the summit for half an hour. A straightforward descent led to the high Marco-e-Rosa Hut, where the process of rehydration began. That evening, after supper, my friend Denise Wilson and two of her daughters unexpectedly arrived at the hut.

Next day, in early morning sunlight, we made an exceptionally enjoyable and beautiful traverse below the peak of Bellavista and over the summits of Piz Palu. Sometimes I really relish doing easy climbs with more time to enjoy the surroundings. We descended to Diavolezza and took a cable car and then a train to our campsite at Morteratsch. Later, we ate out at the cheapest restaurant we could find in Pontresina.

After a pleasant rest day, we decided to attempt the Corda Molla ridge of Monte Disgrazia, a major, rather isolated peak further south in Italy. We drove round into Italy, and reached the road-head at Chiareggio, a charming hamlet. We stopped for a lunchtime pizza, only to be ushered into an immaculate dining room and served a three-course meal. A complex route crossing a rock rib and two different glaciers led up to the Oggione bivouac hut at 3151m, at the foot of our intended climb. The hut was half-cylinder shaped, with a metal exterior and wooden-clad interior, held to its rocky perch by three thick wires. Below was a big drop to the badly crevassed glacier at the foot of the north face. Inside were triple-tiered bunks for twelve, a shelf with some cutlery and a saucepan and a small window above the door.

It started raining heavily in the night, beating on the metallic exterior of the hut. Rain or hail continued all next day. We lay beneath blankets, rising for our meal of bread, ham and cheese. There was no respite in the storm outside. Soon after turning in for the night, there was a huge clap of thunder which shook the entire mountain and, almost immediately, the rain stopped.

We descended in the morning and drove back to Switzerland to camp in the attractive Val Bregaglia at Vicosoprano. That night the storm returned with added fury and part of the campsite was swept away in a mudslide. In the morning there was fresh snow almost to the valley. I was happy to rest and enjoy the flowery meadows but John found it hard to relax and took himself off for a longer walk. Next day we drove back into Italy to the Mello Valley.

The Mello Valley is lined by large granite crags with snowy peaks in the background. We spent a very pleasant day rock climbing on easy angled granite slabs, the sun lighting patches of vivid green grass below, and I thought that Mello was one of the loveliest Alpine valleys I had seen. From the Caesari Ponti Hut, we made a straightforward ascent of the ordinary route on Monte Disgrazia, partly in cloud. Driving back down the valley, we again met the Wilson family. Back at Vicosoprano the campsite was half deserted, with a wintry feel, and in the morning we set off home.

In another good Alpine season, the highlight was definitely the Biancograt.

John Evans on Piz Roseg.

John Evans at the Oggione bivouac hut.

Dent Blanche and Monte Rosa

In August 1989, I had new companions in the Alps, firstly Sarah Howard and then Jay Turner. John Harding introduced me to Sarah, who was an attractive girl, about my age, and due to get married a few weeks later. Her father, who had recently died, was a well known mountaineer in Kenya. Sarah was very keen to climb the Dent Blanche, a route her father had climbed many years previously.

We met in Sion. Sarah and her family were staying with Swiss friends who owned a lovely old, wooden chalet at Ferpècle. Next morning we started out from Arolla. Switzerland looked at its best, with attractive barns, lush green meadows and fine views of the Pigne d'Arolla. We followed the path, marked by red and white paint flashes, towards the Bertol Hut. It was a long walk, the final slopes crossing tiresome soft snow, and the hut itself was reached by a series of metal ladders. Initially the warden was unwelcoming as we had not made a telephone reservation.

Next morning, the granite spire of Aiguille de la Tsa made a good warm-up climb. The rock climbing was excellent but, on the descent, we got caught up in an international pantomime of knitted ropes and jabbering French, with one poor man spread-eagled on an easy angled arête. On the way back to the hut we practised putting on crampons; I was less than pleased to find that Sarah only had old fashioned crampons without front points. The following day we climbed easily to Tête Blanche and crossed snowfields at the head of Val d'Hérens to the Dent Blanche Hut, a traditional Alpine hut.

Sarah and I were first away from the hut at 4.50 in the morning. It wasn't cold, despite clear skies. We followed the rocky rib above the hut and then a snow arête, as a lovely orange dawn spread over the mountains to the east. Three other pairs overtook us before we reached the south ridge proper. We moved together up to the Grand Gendarme. The scenery was wild and grand and the terrain suddenly became more serious, with steep, verglassed rock, protected by metal spikes. I belayed and Sarah led across some difficult slabs, climbing well.

Beyond the Grand Gendarme, the ridge looked most impressive. Soon afterwards one of Sarah's crampons came off. I dreaded to think what might have happened if it had done so a few minutes earlier. We continued, passing another gendarme with awkward climbing on the east side, and a third gendarme on the west, where I was very glad of all the gear I had brought. Although graded PD in our guidebook, to me this climb seemed significantly harder than other PDs such as the Weisshorn or Finsteraahorn. Eventually we passed the worst of the difficulties and a snow arête led up to the summit. It was good to relax and we had the top to ourselves.

On the descent, we avoided many of the difficulties by abseils, taking extreme care. At the foot of the last abseil, I took an ice axe belay. Sarah slipped while down-climbing the snowy gully but I easily held her on the rope. After more down-climbing, at last the difficulties eased and we got back to the hut after exactly twelve hours on the go. Several cups of tea were most welcome but there was little time to relax as we needed to descend to the valley.

Not far below the hut we lost the route and were forced to cross a couple of strong glacial streams. It was a lovely evening, with shafts of sunlight coming through the jagged rock ridge above and blue-green shadows in the valley below, which looked a long way down. With squelching boots, we continued on down the path towards Ferpècle. The final part, through the woods, seemed to go on and on and I walked in an almost dream-like state. We reached the chalet at 9.00pm.

After breakfast next morning, I was told that it was 'not the plan of the house' that I should stay any longer. Sarah and her mother drove me to Les Haudères, where we parted. It seemed an abrupt end to our trip. I found a hotel and sorted my kit, enjoying the sun but feeling a little lonely. Jay arrived two mornings later. We met in Visp, took the bus to Saas Almagell and walked up to the modern Almegeller Hut. I felt fit and relaxed and found Jay's friendly company quite a relief. Sarah had an intense curiosity about everything, constantly asking questions, which I found quite tiring after a time.

Next day we traversed the Weissmies, mostly on rock going up, and on snow descending. I remember it as a very enjoyable day. As we climbed, we had beautiful views to the east, with many shades of light, and range after range of peaks. We could see as far as the Bernina Alps and Monte Disgrazia.

The following day, we traversed the Fletschhorn and Lagginhorn. We got lost for a frustrating hour in the pre-dawn, clambering around on scree, until we could see the correct route. There was some cloud and none of the beauty of the previous day's views. In fact, it was raining by the time we returned to the hut. We walked on down the valley and then descended by téléphérique, a wise decision as it seemed a very long way down.

Back at Pension Edelweiss in Saas Almagell, I managed to talk Jay into a rest day. We enjoyed the views, the flowers on our shaded balcony and the cuisine. We discussed the plan and decided to make an ambitious traverse of Monte Rosa by the Cresta Signal.

So, next day, we took a bus to the large earth-dam at the head of the valley and walked beside the Mattmark lake, then plodded wearily up to the Monte Moro pass, where there was a great view of the north-east face of Monte Rosa. We descended by téléphérique to Macugnaga. The valley looked green and attractive, with a large old church, and we found a good *ristorante* for lunch. Two chairlifts and a half-hour's walk took us to the Zambone e Zappa Hut.

We woke to a view of the sun already catching the top of Monte Rosa and left at 7.45am after Jay performed a last-minute re-pack. A long and difficult glacier climb with intricate route-finding led to a col, and a rocky ridge continued over the Punta Tre Amici. Jay moved quite slowly. I tried to be patient but the rope was often tight. The Resegotti bivouac hut was a small wooden building with metal-clad roof. There were blankets and even a stove. We had it to ourselves until two climbers came in very quietly during the night.

We started up the Cresta Signal as the sky began to lighten at 5.45am. There were frequent strange flashes of lightning away to the south but clear skies with moon and stars overhead. The first part of the route was along easy rock ledges on the south side of the ridge. As we made progress up the broken rocks, a helicopter buzzed around and landed people below the face on our right. We guessed they were looking for bodies and, sadly, this was confirmed later.

We put on crampons for some snow crests and kept them on for the mixed ground above. The climbing was quite hard and sustained but the belays were good. Jay was climbing well and it was nice to be in the sun. It was strange to climb a route with a hut, the Margherita Hut, near the top. We could see it getting steadily closer, rope-length by rope-length. Crampon scratches showed the line up gullies and chimneys, mostly on the south side of the ridge. It was a long climb and we finally reached the top at 4.00pm. Fifteen minutes of easy cramponing led to the hut at the summit of Signalkuppe. The evening meal cost £16, about a pound a mouthful, but the view of the Matterhorn and the sunset behind shifting clouds more than compensated. I felt that the Cresta Signal had been one of my best Alpine routes. It was certainly the most serious Alpine climb that Jay and I did together and I have happy memories of it.

In the morning, we decided to continue our expedition by traversing over the Liskamm. We found it quite straightforward, despite Jay's concerns about a double cornice, and I was glad we made the effort. From the Felikjoch we descended on the Swiss side, down the Zwillings Glacier – I enjoyed the challenge of finding a route through the icefall at the bottom – and took the Gornergrat railway to Zermatt. We ended the day back at Visp with a bath, clean clothes and a good evening meal.

Sarah Howard on the Aiguille de la Tsa.

View east from the Weissmies.

Jay on the Cresta Signal.

Gran Paradiso and Grandes Jorasses

The start of our Alpine season in August 1993 was easily the worst ever. Jay and I, now engaged after my return from the Far East, flew out to the Alps for a week in the Gran Paradiso area. We couldn't find accommodation anywhere at Cogne and eventually, in desperation, we took the bus back to Aosta and spent the first night in a motel beside the motorway. Things could only improve after that and we spent a few nights at the Sella Hut. The peaks were not memorable but we enjoyed the wildlife, seeing lots of ibex and chamois, and we delighted in the flowers.

I felt more in tune with the mountains once we moved to the quieter Val Savarenche. From the modern Chabod Hut we made a straightforward ascent of the Gran Paradiso. We dropped down to the Victor Emmanuel Hut, which has a distinctive, round, metal roof. It was crowded but the staff coped with efficiency and good humour. After a restful morning, we made a traverse back to the Chabod Hut, with great views of the Gran Paradiso. Next day, we continued to traverse, crossing a col on a rock ridge and descending by clinging to metal chains. We saw marmots and lots of ibex and had an exceptionally beautiful walk down to the wooded valley in the bright afternoon sun.

For the second week that year, I met up with John Evans in Courmayeur, for what turned out to be our last Alpine holiday together. We started by going up from Planpincieux to the Boccalette Hut for the ordinary route on the Grandes Jorasses. The hut walk was more like a scramble: two and a half hours of unremitting uphill grind, but for once I beat John. The hut was a small wooden building beside a tumbling icefall. It had only three rooms and there were just a few other climbers.

We left at 3.30am. The glacier above was much steeper than I expected but to be amid such spectacular scenery by moonlight was quite awe-inspiring. At the Rocher du Reposoir, in the half-light, we climbed difficult rocks with strenuous chimneys and grooves. At the top of the rock rib we crossed another steep and exposed glacier to reach the Rocher Whymper. Our guidebook described this spur as 'easy, broken rocks'. They were anything but, and we moved one at a time, rope-length by rope-length.

The summit of Pointe Whymper was a great viewpoint but we were concerned by the look of the traverse to Pointe Walker, the highest summit. This was some of the most frightening mountaineering I had done, with cornices on the French side and, on the Italian side, steep, rotten ice which fell away with each blow of the axe. We had very dry mouths by the time we reached the summit. We descended on snow, with extreme care, and then retraced our route to the hut, returning fourteen and a half hours after starting.

Although the scenery had been magnificent, I found the climb just too stressful to be fully enjoyable.

Two days later, we climbed the Tour Ronde and then crossed the Vallée Blanche to the Cosmiques Hut. We were all set for Mont Blanc and the evening was fine. Maddeningly, next morning there was cloud and wind. We climbed the Cosmiques Arête as a consolation route and descended to Chamonix.

The Grandes Jorasses was the last of the great climbs I made in the Alps, which had started with the Wetterhorn twelve years earlier. Jay and I continued to return most summers. We had many great holidays and climbed good routes, including 4000m peaks, but never with quite the intensity of those early years.

Jay above the Sella Hut. Grivola in the background.

Sunrise from the Grandes Jorasses.

John Evans at the summit of the Grandes Jorasses.

Office Dreams

From my overheated office block
Where I sit and stare and watch the clock,
I think of mountains in the sunrise glow
And the crunch of crampons on frozen snow.

I wish I was back at an Alpine hut,
Looking outside at the next day's route,
Setting out in the starry night,
Climbing up to the sun and the light
Putting on sun-cream, uncoiling the rope,
Kicking steps up the icy slope,
Precious moments of summit content,
Endless caution on the long descent.

Back to the hut for some much-needed brews
Before lying outside for an afternoon snooze
Until I wake up with a sudden jerk
And realize it's time to get on with my work.

(RH, WRITTEN IN 1984)

ELEVEN

Greenland

In May 1984, I took part in an Eagle Ski Club expedition to Mont Forel in East Greenland, led by Derek Fordham, an architect and very experienced Arctic traveller. Mont Forel is located on the edge of the icecap, at an altitude of 3383m, and is one of the highest mountains in Greenland, the highest being Gunnsbjørn Fjell (3699m). The other members were Graham Elson and Mike Esten, both in their forties, and David Waldron, close to me in age.

Our aim was to make a lightweight ski approach from the coast, having air-dropped food boxes below Mont Forel and at the half-way point. Sadly the weather had other ideas and we were delayed for five frustrating days in Iceland before our chartered Twin Otter flew us to Kulusuk airstrip. Low cloud still prevented the airdrops and, after two more days, we were forced to make a radical revision to our plans. We decided to charter a helicopter to make the inland journey.

Two days later, we finally made the flight and it surpassed all expectations. First, we had a great view of the frozen fjords, then we landed to refuel at Sermiligâq, where most of the village's children came out and clustered around the helicopter. Soon afterwards, we landed to drop a food depot at the Knud Rasmussen Glacier. I was astonished at the size of the glaciers, which utterly dwarfed those in Switzerland. As we flew on, the scenery became more and more spectacular, with fine granite peaks, rock buttresses and spires. We left more food boxes at a col below Conniat Bjerg and flew up the Paris Gletscher and the Bjørnegletscher, until suddenly we were flying past the steep walls of Mont Forel.

We piled out and soon the helicopter left, leaving the air full of tiny ice crystals. It was -18°C. Mont Forel looked impressive. Throughout the long planning evenings in the basement of Derek's Greenwich home, I had always expressed confidence about climbing the peak. Now I wasn't quite so sure!

In the morning we left camp quite late, after some rifle practice. Polar bears are unlikely but not completely unknown so far inland. Distances were deceptive in the clear air and it took longer to reach the mountain than I expected. We cramponed up to a col on the south-west ridge. There were great views to the south. Above was steep, mixed ground and after a short time Derek, Graham and Mike decided to retreat. David and I continued for several rope-lengths of enjoyable, mixed climbing at about a 45 degree angle. Eventually, we reached the foot of a large rock buttress and, with little equipment and short of time, we decided to turn back. It was a spectacular spot, with range after range of peaks to the south, the icecap extending away to the north and the tiny specks of our tents below.

Next day we skied around the north ridge of Mont Forel to reconnoitre the easiest looking route, which I had spotted from the helicopter and had also noted from books at Derek's home. A long snow slope led up to the south-east ridge, which appeared to have a gentler angle than the others. This was the ridge climbed by André Roch's Swiss party in 1939, although they accessed it from the south. Next morning I was cursed for getting everyone up at 4.15am but it was the right decision; it was a fine morning and we still weren't away until 6.15am.

As we skied around the north ridge, the wind increased strongly, blowing a snow plume off the summit. David and I decided to reconnoitre the route anyway. After a long climb and some difficulties, we finally reached the high col. The spindrift had become extremely unpleasant and we both started having trouble seeing. From the little we could see, the final 300m or so looked quite straightforward. We started to retreat immediately, rope-length by rope-length, with ice axe belays.

Conditions worsened. I had already ripped off my glasses but my whole face was just a mass of icicles and my eyelids started to freeze up. David was in a worse way and could hardly see anything. I started getting terrible cramp in both legs. Down and down we went; at first the rest on the stances was welcome but the wind was increasing, blowing spindrift directly up the slope, which itself was a mass of sliding snow. I was getting very cold and, as the belays were largely psychological, we moved down together, David in front, nearly blind, and me shouting 'left, right, down'.

I kept hoping that the wind would calm down but it didn't. We never even saw the bergschrund! We fairly ran the last 300m to the skis. The situation was getting desperate: David was complaining of frostbitten hands. We grabbed the skis and ran down to a small hollow giving some shelter at the very bottom of the slope. I tried warming David's hands in mine and pulled out my spare socks. Meanwhile one of his gloves blew off up the hill. I got my duvet out, made David put up his hood, and took off both pairs of crampons, David's hands being useless. On with the skis, but as soon as we got round the corner it was obvious we would have a major battle as the wind was coming directly down the slope.

Again we stopped to try to warm David's hands and I gave him my overgloves. We had to keep going to get back to camp but the col looked far away and the wind was so strong that we had to zigzag up at 45 degrees. David kept going well but we both got blown over. My eyelids were again freezing but I could just see the col through gaps in the spindrift. Somehow we made it; immediately beyond the north ridge there was much more shelter, although we could hear the roar of the wind high on the peak. Finally we reached the tents and I was bundled in with Mike, who was very welcoming to such a snowy, bedraggled figure.

David developed badly blistered fingers from frostbite and Derek decided that we should leave for the coast as soon as the weather permitted. Two days later, we skied, roped, down the Bjørn pass, which was difficult with heavy packs, and we all fell occasionally. As we descended, the weather became much warmer and we had good views of Chamonix-like rock peaks on either side of the glacier.

The next two days were disappointing as the views were mostly obscured by mist. Skiing along on a compass-bearing with heavy packs, sore heels and aching shoulders, longing for the five minutes per hour rest break, was little fun. Eventually the weather improved and we had a glorious evening for a key climb of an icefall to reach our half-way food boxes at Conniats Pass. The boxes were nearly covered in snow.

Two more days of gentle skiing down wide glaciers took us to our pick-up point at the end of the Knud Rasmussen Glacier and, thirty-six hours late due to more bad weather, the helicopter arrived. We flew back to Iceland the next day.

On the return flight to Heathrow, I reflected on the expedition. The Arctic was an extremely beautiful but austere place and I decided I preferred the softer, more varied Alpine landscape, where forests and flowery meadows provide a contrast to the snow peaks. But it had been a terrific experience and one I certainly didn't regret.

Our first view of Mont Forel from the helicopter.

Camp below Mont Forel.

Derek approaching Conniats Pass.

At our food depot at Conniats Pass.

Twelve

The Pyrenees
in Winter

In March 1985, I was invited to join a ski-tour in the Pyrenees led by John Harding. John was in his early fifties, a solicitor working in the City of London. He had previously worked as a political officer in South Arabia. At the time, he was one of the country's leading amateur ski-mountaineers and was more than half-way to completing, over a number of seasons, the first British winter traverse of the Pyrenees from Pic d'Anie in the west to Canigou in the east.

The tour in 1985 was, for me, the first of three Pyrenean trips with John. I also joined him on tours to the Picos de Europa, the Sierra de Gredos, the Sierra Cantábrica and Corsica. John was very erudite, with exceptional historical and cultural knowledge, but he had an affable leadership style and a great sense of humour. There was always a lot of friendly banter on these trips. I think we recognized in each other a similar drive to achieve the next mountain objective. Perhaps my main contribution was to provide enthusiasm. Certainly, I was grateful to be invited back, time after time, and greatly enjoyed these years of exploratory ski-mountaineering under John's leadership.

Winter touring in the Pyrenees, back in the 1980s, was in many ways more serious than Alpine touring. There were few guidebooks and the red *Editorial Alpina* Spanish maps provided only an approximation of the terrain, with few contours and no cliffs. The huts were mainly unguarded and primitive, the mountains are steep and avalanche-prone, without easy glacier highways, and the weather is often poor.

The party in 1985 consisted of John Harding, Roger Childs, Julian Lush, Patrick Bailey, David Seddon and me. Roger was a company director living in Greenwich and was to become a good friend over the following years. He was the first to admit that he was no great mountaineer but he more than made up for it with his strength and good humour. Julian was a former Shell manager and an old Wykehamist, Patrick an accountant and editor of the Eagle Ski Club Yearbook, and David was a doctor, about a year older than me.

We met in the elegant spa town of Bagnères-de-Luchon and set out, rather late, the following morning, with an ambitious plan to cross the frontier ridge into Spain and reach the Rencluse Hut in the Esera valley. We climbed difficult slopes with heavy packs in blazing sun, snow sticking to our skis and sweat stinging our eyes. By the time we reached Pic de Roye in mid-afternoon, it was clear we had no chance of completing the day's plan. Providentially we spotted a small hut about 300m below which provided very primitive shelter for the night.

The next morning was fine with beautiful sunlight and views. We soon retraced our steps and continued along an interesting ridge towards the frontier, with one short descent on foot. From the Port de la Picarde, we had a great view of the Maladeta massif opposite and we could see the Rencluse Hut part way up the slope. We skied down to the pine trees in the valley, where John waxed eloquent about 'the quintessential essence of the Spanish Pyrenees'. It was a hot slog up to the hut, which was closed, but we installed ourselves in the winter quarters next door. That night, the stars were very bright and we seemed well set for Pico d'Aneto next day.

We rose at 6.00am but, by the time we finished breakfast, it was snowing. The snow developed into a blizzard for the rest of the day and I spent most of the time in my sleeping bag to keep warm. It continued to snow all night and was still snowing in the morning, so John decided to retreat. The avalanche danger was high until we reached the valley and then it was arduous work, trail-breaking downhill through the deep snow. A long, hard descent ended with a 4km road walk in the rain to Benasque. We found accommodation in the Hotel Barrabés and Roger, who spoke fluent Spanish, came into his own organizing a most welcome tapas meal within minutes.

Those first three days of Pyrenean touring were like a microcosm of many of our Spanish tours: tough, often in poor weather but occasionally brilliant. A detailed account is published in John Harding's book *Pyrenean High Route*. That year I only had one week's leave booked and, rather sadly, bade farewell to the team on the edge of the Aigües Tortes National Park.

In 1988, I joined the final leg of John's long saga. For the first part, we had some truly terrible weather, skiing on snow-covered roads over the Col de Puymorens, on the edge of Andorra, in a complete blizzard. I remember seeing Roger, a large man, lifted into the air and blown over by the wind outside a primitive hut called Maison des Ingénieurs in the Lanoux valley. Another retreat followed the next day.

During the second part of the tour, the weather finally improved. We traversed Puigmal to reach Núria, a Spanish valley head with abbey church and small ski-resort, and next day continued to the Ull de Terr Hut. The following day we covered over 20km, travelling fast on hard, sastrugi snow along a high ridge. Unfortunately, our intended destination, the Pla Guillem Hut, was completely full of snow. We descended 500m to the Marialles Hut, expecting another uncomfortable night, only to find a delightful, newly renovated building with a fireplace, chairs and tables and a fine evening view of Canigou.

Sleep was fitful, with a cacophony of snoring, and we started early next morning in fine weather, following a forest track and then climbing more open slopes. Rounding a corner, we had our first close-up view of Canigou, an impressive rock peak with a long, crenellated ridge above a steep wall on the left, and a couloir splitting the face and providing the easiest looking line, on the right. David Williams and I were ahead and, swapping skis for crampons, we continued to a small col, chatting about Alpine climbing. The col was an impressive spot and, in the distance, we could see the coastline near Perpignan.

We continued up the broad, steep gully, which had beautiful ice frostings on the rocks. Near the top, we stood aside to let John attack the final pitch with his alpenstock, then dropped the rope for Roger and David Seddon. Soon we all stood on the summit, which was a magnificent viewpoint and doubtless an emotional moment for John.

We cramponed down ice-feathered snow just left of the crest of the north ridge and then skied down to the trees in burning hot sun. Our adventures were not quite over, however. It's never a good idea to follow David Williams on skis. Going at high speed down a forest track, David made a playful little jump at one of the sharp corners. Trying to follow, I caught an edge and flew off the side of the track. A rather bruised and battered Rupert was retrieved from about 5m down the steep hillside. It could easily have been much worse! We continued to ski slowly to the snowline, and then walked down the path in glorious evening sunlight, finally reaching a rather unwelcoming bar in Fillols.

Canigou was a fitting climax to John's long journey. However, we returned to the Pyrenees the next year to climb Pico de Posets and Pico d'Aneto, two of the major summits which had eluded John earlier. Both gave excellent three-day tours and outstanding views.

John Harding in the Sierra de Gredos.

Approaching Pic de Roye.

Roger Childs and David Seddon on Pic de la Mounjoye.

David Williams and John Harding at the Marialles Hut.

Simon Kirk on Pico de Posets.

Thirteen

Ski-touring
in Spain

Picos de Europa

The Picos de Europa is a compact range of limestone peaks on the northern edge of the Cantabrian Mountains, near Santander on the north coast of Spain. Deep gorges with huge rock walls divide the range into a western, central and eastern massif. In February 1986, John Harding invited me to join a group for a week's ski-touring. The others were Roger Childs, David Seddon and Derek Fordham.

We started from the village of Espinama, where we found a small hotel with smoky bar and the ubiquitous television. The village was attractive, with all the roofs covered in deep snow. A day tour showed us that the mountains had exceptional snow that year and it was soon obvious that our planned traverse across the range was out of the question, due to the steep terrain and avalanche danger.

We made some pleasant tours, exploring around the edges of the highest mountain areas, staying at rustic villages. One day we set out from Fuente Dé, at the foot of a magnificent cirque with enormous vertical cliffs of pale-coloured limestone. Every branch of every tree was laden with snow and, with this spectacular backdrop, we took a lot of photographs. The afternoon became very hot and the snow was sticking, infuriatingly, to the base of the skis. In a fit of temper, trying to dislodge the snow, I hit my skis so hard that my ski pole snapped.

Another day, we skied down into the Cares Gorge, an exceptionally deep ravine with tremendous rock walls. At the bar at Caín, a small hamlet, we had beer and ate the local *jamon* (dry cured ham) and chorizo, before climbing back out of the gorge to Posada de Valdeón. A couple of days later we took a Land Rover taxi round to Covadonga. The driver showed us two jagged holes in the wing, acquired the previous day: stray bullets from a local hunter. At Cangas de Onis we admired a fine Roman bridge, its arches framing the snowy background peaks.

Covadonga has a large Cathedral, a monastery and a big hotel, where we secured accommodation, as the only visitors, and tucked into a good lunch. In the afternoon, John and I walked up a ridge above the hotel. It was fine and sunny, and the views of the snow-plastered mountains improved with every step. I went far further than I originally intended but wet feet from walking in snow was a small price to pay for one of those periods of fantastic light and happiness that occur only once or twice a year.

Next day, we skied to a hut at Lago Enol and to a small summit above. The hut would be a good base for future ski-touring but our time was up. We skied down to the snowline next morning, where a pre-arranged taxi was waiting – the end of an interesting week exploring the 'lost' valleys and gorges of the Picos under heavy snow.

Sierra de Gredos

During our Pyrenean tour in 1986, Roger Childs said more than once that we should visit the Sierra de Gredos with skis. We were sceptical at first but we should have known better, particularly as Roger owned a house on the south side of the range. In February 1988 we took action and Roger, John Harding, Derek Fordham and I flew to Spain for a long weekend.

The Sierra de Gredos is an east-west trending range of granitic mountains near the centre of Spain, about 150km west of Madrid, separating the provinces of Castilla y León and Castilla-La Mancha. The highest peak is Almanzor (2592m), named after the famous Moorish general. It was late at night when we arrived at Roger's property, Prado Lobero, above the town of Candeleda. Next morning, in bright sunlight, we admired the beautiful twin-roofed farmhouse with its mellow stone walls and ochre roof tiles. Snow-capped mountains dominated the background and there was an extensive view over the Tagus river valley to the south.

Access to the Sierra de Gredos is easiest from the north, as the south side of the range is steep and remote. We drove round to the north by the Puerto de Tornavacas and from the road-head at Plataforma we skinned up to the nearby Llano hut. The winter quarters were quite Spartan but later in the evening the guardian arrived and we moved into the main hut, where I wrote my diary by the light of a log fire. It was a very noisy night as one party of Spaniards after another arrived for the weekend.

In the morning, we skinned steadily up to the ridge and traversed along to the summit of La Mira (2343m). This short ski-tour was one of the most beautiful I ever remember. The low sun was glinting off the icy snow, casting long shadows, and the views were fabulous, especially to the south where mist lay in the Tagus valley.

Next day, we climbed to the ridge above the Circo de Gredos, which is the most spectacular corrie of the range, with summer and winter climbing, and dropped down to the Elola Hut by the Laguna Grande. Some of the others were suffering from sore feet and second-day lethargy but, after some coffee, I persuaded them to set out for Almanzor while the going was good.

We zigzagged at a steep angle on skins and then climbed a long gully on foot up to the Portilla de los Cobardes. Small lumps of ice were melting from the rocks and raining down. I found a gully that led to the summit; although the final ten feet were difficult, luckily there were handholds just when they were needed. I touched the trig point and went down to offer a rope for the others. Just at that moment, John and Derek were hit by some falling ice and decided to retreat. Some great skiing back to the hut rounded off a memorable day. The hut was quiet once the weekend hordes departed.

The weather was less settled the next morning and, after a short tour, we retreated to a Parador hotel for lunch. From the north, the Sierra de Gredos looked very reminiscent of the Cairngorms. We drove back to Roger's home and went out for another Parador meal, where we were joined by Julia Kemp, a well-known wildlife film maker.

The Gredos exceeded all expectations and we returned the following year. Unfortunately the weather was poor and I developed flu-like symptoms which Roger treated with an extremely effective powder he purchased in Candeleda. The highlight, for me, was a quick visit to Avila en route to Roger's home. The massive walls seemed to have a magical quality in the bright moonlight.

A third visit to the Gredos for a week in 1998 was much more productive, although a very high snowline and bitterly cold wind put paid to our hopes of making a traverse of the whole range. This time the team was Roger, Jay Turner, Mike Daley and me. Roger had an enormous range of interests and talents and was an exceptionally kind and charming person. By now, we had become good friends. Sadly he died in 2010.

The trip began with an extremely enjoyable day tour to the Sierra de Béhar, an isolated massif west of the Gredos. We set out from a road-head at 1600m, above the picturesque village of Candelario with its steep cobbled streets and wrought-iron balconies. After an hour of carrying skis, we continued on skins. Every blade of grass was coated in thick ice crystals glinting in the bright sun. We skied over the highest summit, Canchal La Ceja (2340m) and continued to the finer summit of Calvitero (2401m). The last section had a sting in the tail, known as the Devil's Step, which was protected by a thick steel cable.

The Western Gredos is dominated by a triple-topped peak called Covacha. The views from Calvitero convinced us that this was not a ski peak but we wanted to climb it anyway, so next morning we arranged a Land Rover lift up the rough, steep dirt roads to about 1400m. The driver worked as a ranger for the Regional Park Authority and was responsible for protecting the *capra hispanica* (mountain ibex) from poachers. He came with us until high on the ridge before dropping down to a valley to the south with a suspiciously large rucksack. A magnificent eagle soared overhead as we walked up the broom-covered slopes. Once on the snow, we needed crampons as the surface was rock hard. Mike and I reached the western summit just before our self-imposed 3.00pm deadline. We had a long descent to Puerto de Tornavacas, fully exposed to the bitter north-east wind, and reached the road in fading light after a strenuous nine-and-a-half-hour day.

It was clear that a ski-traverse to the Central Gredos was impractical so, after a cultural day in Avila, we skied the following day from Plataforma to Morezón. The wind had finally subsided and we had a good view of the Circo de Gredos. Sadly, the day was spoiled when Roger sprained his ankle in a fall near the very end of the descent.

In another change of plan, the three of us decided to cross the range on foot and descend on the south side, where Roger would meet us. First we had an interesting climb to La Galana, the second highest summit of the range, before dropping down to the Elola Hut. Next morning we crossed the main range and, after a lengthy glissade, left the snow behind. Our route lay down a granite ridge, with occasional tors and splendid views of the snow-capped peaks above, and we saw some *capra hispanica*. Eventually, after a long descent, we reached a forest road and half an hour later we successfully met Roger at the Refugio del Concal. As we wandered around the olive groves and orchard at Roger's *finca* next day, I reflected on a terrifically enjoyable week.

Sierra Cantábrica

The Picos de Europa form only a small part of a much bigger range of mountains in the north of Spain. In February 1992, while home on leave from the Far East, I joined a tour led by John Harding to explore some of this range. The team consisted of John, Roger Childs, Richard Morgan, Derek Fordham, Jay Turner, Simon Kirk, John Hayward and me. John Hayward was a younger recruit. He was employed as an aid-worker in Afghanistan and had grown a large beard to help him blend in with the locals.

This was the ski-tour with no skis! A glimpse of the mountains from the Parador hotel at Cervera de Pisuerga showed there was clearly inadequate snow for skiing. We undertook the tour anyway, using a combination of training shoes and ski boots. Only John Hayward carried skis. We made an ascent of Curavacas (2520m) from a campsite in a valley below. John Hayward and I chose a steep snow gully between walls of conglomerate rock and, kicking steps up the gully, I felt happier than at any time in the past few months in Indonesia. Easier scrambling led to the summit, where we rejoined the others.

Two days later, we climbed Peña Prieta (2536m), another rewarding peak. The scenery reminded me of parts of north-west Scotland on a good day at Easter time. We had some fine glissading on the descent. Next day, we continued, with our camping gear, over a col and, after walking down a road for a few kilometres, we were pleased to come across a small inn, Pension Espigüete. Roger soon organized a meal of fried eggs, chips and chorizo.

Espigüete (2450m), the third main peak of the area, which looks very similar to Ben Lui, was our next objective. Splitting into two parties, the two Johns and I climbed the central gully while the others climbed the east ridge. Our face was less steep than it looked and we reached the top without difficulty. The descent was by a long scree slope on the south side, a complete contrast to the snowy north. A track through old oak trees took us back to our base.

The following day we had a cultural break, visiting León. In the bright sun, the fine Gothic cathedral, with its double flying buttresses and pale sandstone, was very memorable. Unusually, I enjoyed it as much as the mountains. We also inspected the cloisters of the Convent of San Marcos and found time for a late Parador lunch. Next day we re-visited the Cares Gorge in the Picos de Europa before heading off to Bilbao. Despite the lack of enough snow for skiing, the week in the Sierra Cantábrica with a friendly group had been delightful.

John Harding in the Picos de Europa. Spectacular scenery but not ideal for ski-touring.

John Harding and Roger Childs near the summit of La Mira in the Sierra de Gredos.

In the Sierra de Gredos. (I lost my beard soon after my 30th birthday!)

On Curavacas.

Fourteen

Corsica

Summer

Books and guides made Corsica sound an attractive destination and in June 1988 Jay Turner and I decided to visit for a rock climbing holiday. Jay and I had already climbed together on frequent weekends over the last two years. We started our holiday at a campsite below the citadel in Corte and, next day, drove to a road-head beyond Calacuccia. Shouldering monstrous packs, we walked slowly up the track, admiring the Cinque Frati towers above, and camped by a stream amid some fine pine trees. With a chill wind, a heavy shower and some thunder rumbling around the hills, it seemed very different from the heat in Corte that morning.

The next morning we climbed Capu Tighiettu. Our route involved almost continuous scrambling up fine red rock. There were many flowers and we learnt to avoid touching the prickly, shrubby vegetation. Near the summit we met a herd of wild goats and had a sudden view of the great rock tooth of Paglia Orba through a gap in the clouds. Back at our campsite, we had a refreshing swim in a deep pool in the stream.

The following day we set off to climb the Finch Route on Paglia Orba. As we climbed up the Paglia Orba Ravine, the peak glowed red and looked ever more impressive. We scrambled up a long rock rib to gain the start of the climbing. Several pitches, some with hard, strenuous moves, led up to the Via Finch. This extraordinary ledge led across the face, rising from right to left. Astonishingly, it was first climbed by George Finch with his brother Max and Norwegian friend Bryn in the winter of 1908. What a climber George Finch must have been!

At the end of the Via Finch, an awkward chimney led up to the Brèche des Anglais, and, above, the south-east ridge gave some delightful climbing, with two sustained pitches. A short scramble led to the summit cross and I said to

Jay that it had been one of the best rock climbs I had done. We descended chimneys through strange, agglomeratic rock and then took the GR20 path down to the pine forests. Back at the tent, restored by a swim and some food, I looked up at the peak with evening cloud swirling around. It was hard to believe that we had climbed right up there.

The next day I was all for a rest day, enjoying our delightful forest campsite, but Jay was having none of it. I was dragged, rather sulkily I must admit, to climb the Cinque Frati. We scrambled up the Ravin de Quarcetta, an impressive gorge, to the start of the route. Several sustained pitches led to the summit of Tower 1 and I looked down on the red roofs of Calasima and wondered whether I wouldn't rather be there. We carried on over Towers 2, 3 and 4. Jay took every opportunity to study the guidebooks in three languages but the easiest line was generally obvious. A long abseil from Tower 5 took us down to easy ground and we returned late to the tent.

In the morning, we finally had a half-rest day before walking out to Calacuccia. We continued to explore Corsica, walking up Capu d'Orto, swimming in the sea at Porto and visiting the citadel at Calvi. The island certainly lived up to our expectations and Jay and I have warm memories of our first summer climbing holiday together.

Winter

I returned to Corsica in February 1994, on a ski-tour led by John Harding. With us were Patrick Fagan, Rodney Franklin, David Williams and Steve Baker, a strong Alpine Ski Club team. The plan was to make a south-to-north traverse of the northern part of the GR20 route.

At Ajaccio, we managed to catch the train by hailing it beside the track, waving our ski sticks. We wound inland, the snow peaks getting closer, and emerged from a long tunnel to disembark at Vizzavona. The scenery was very fine, with beautiful pine trees and rugged granite peaks, but the snow looked a long way off.

We shouldered heavy packs, with skis added, and set off along the GR20 path, which was well marked with red and white paint flashes. After about an hour, we rested on some rock slabs by a waterfall, enjoying the spring crocuses. The path climbed more steeply and at about 1325m we put on skis and made a steep climb to a col at about 2000m. It was slow, hot, thirsty work, with sweat stinging the eyes, but from the top we had a good view of Monte Rotondo and there was a slight breeze. After a hard first day, a difficult ski descent on crusty snow took us to the Onda Hut. Like all the huts in Corsica, it was unguarded in winter.

Next morning, we rose early in the hope of cooler weather. We climbed to a ridge, first on foot and then on skis. There was a sea of cloud below to the east and a good sunrise over a jagged rock ridge. The ridge narrowed and we made a steep traverse below the crest, tackling several sections on foot. We reached the Petra Piana Hut after seven hours of strenuous ski-mountaineering.

The following day we climbed Monte Rotondo, mostly on crampons due to the icy snow. The summit was a great viewpoint. To the north, we could see the massif of Monte Cinto and the unmistakable shape of Paglia Orba; to the west was Capu d'Orto, where Jay and I had walked above Porto; to the east was a sea of cloud, and to the south a view of impressive peaks including Monte d'Oro. Back at the hut, we were joined by a solitary Frenchman, Laurent, who came with us for the next few days.

The Manganu Hut was our destination the next day and we crossed various cols and steep traverses to reach it. That night, the stars were as brilliant as I could ever remember. Next morning began with a descent, followed by a climb through beautiful scenery, the pine trees framing views of snowy peaks. We dropped down towards Verghio, reaching a forest track which led to the road and the Castel di Verghio Hotel. I was ahead at this point and wondered why the others didn't appear. Sadly, Steve had torn his knee ligaments and the others were helping him up to the road. The hotel was full but Laurent found us accommodation in a private hut, where the locals plied us with alcohol and food. It was a strange end to an eventful day.

In the morning Steve departed by ambulance. I felt very sorry for him, remembering how lonely I felt on leaving the party during my first tour in the Pyrenees. The rest of us walked north up the GR20 path, stopping for lunch at a lovely spot by a waterfall with tremendous cliffs of orange granite above. Soon afterwards, we were able to put on skis and a few hundred metres of skinning led to the Mori Hut. Next morning, we climbed Paglia Orba, cramponing up hard-frozen névé in the gully that Jay and I had descended six years earlier. We then skied down the Foggiale valley and continued on foot to the Tighiettu Hut.

The weather remained fine for our ascent of Monte Cinto (2706m), Corsica's highest peak. We cramponed up steep slopes for two and a half hours. It was hard work, carrying heavy skis, but a great view opened up of range after range in different shades of blue to the south-west. A long ridge led on to the summit, which was slightly marred by the remains of a building. One by one, the party staggered up and we took group photographs.

We skied down to the south on soft snow, losing hundreds of feet in only a few minutes of pure enjoyment. Eventually we reached a stream where some of the team took a refreshing dip. Long, dry slopes of maquis scrub led endlessly down to the valley. The afternoon turned to a fine evening, with blossom on the fruit trees and the silhouette of the Cinque Frati ridge above, and we reached the bar at Calacuccia at 6.00pm.

We had completed the first British ski-traverse of the Corsican High Level Route and, back in Ajaccio, we were reunited with Steve. Though I had found the initial days quite strenuous, I really enjoyed the final part of the tour. On our flight to Paris, we had a brilliant view of all the summits we had climbed and, a few minutes later, extensive views of the Alpes Maritimes, Monte Viso and the whole of the western Alps.

Laurent, our French companion, on Monte Cinto, with a view to Paglia Orba.

Paglia Orba in summer.

The Corsica winter team: (L–R) David Williams, Rodney Franklin, John Harding, me, Steve Baker and Patrick Fagan.

FIFTEEN

Tysfjord and Lofoten

The Arctic Highway south-west of Narvik passes through a relatively low-lying and uninteresting area beyond Ballangen; then, suddenly, on rounding a corner, the whole dramatic profile of the Tysfjord mountains is revealed. These stark, ice-sculpted granitic peaks rise so abruptly that they look quite unreal, as if part of a fantasy landscape. The road passes between the precipices of Stortinden to the north and Huglehornet to the south. Here John Evans and I left the bus; our long journey was at an end.

We had both decided we needed a change from the Alps for our summer holiday in 1986. We chose to travel to Norway and spend one week in Tysfjord and one week in Lofoten. I had always wanted to visit the Lofoten Islands, ever since seeing their jagged profile in the distance from a peak near Narvik eleven years earlier. As before, we took the train from Stockholm. By the time we stepped out of the bus, we certainly felt a long way from home. Indeed, John remarked that it had taken considerably less time to reach Kashmir.

Our first objective was the east ridge of Huglehornet. We reached the foot of the ridge by walking easily up an extraordinary slab of granite gneiss set at an angle of about 25 degrees. This single slab was about half a kilometre long and several hundred metres wide: a unique feature. At the foot of the ridge, 'the party' fell noticeably silent. The narrow rock ridge rose at a steep angle to a huge capping overhang. Had we not known in advance that the grade was only V Diff/Severe, I expect we would have made an excuse to find an easier-looking objective. As it was, the climb was highly enjoyable and the summit a tremendous viewpoint. The weather was perfect and all around we could see fjords, islands and fine peaks. There is a special magic about the combination of mountains and the sea. In the distance we could see the Lofoten Islands and to the south-east was the unmistakeable profile of Stetind.

Stetind (the Anvil Peak) is one of the most distinctive mountains in Norway. It has the shape of a very steep-sided triangular pyramid with a flat top. Described by Priestman as 'probably the most remarkable and at the same time the ugliest mountain in Arctic Norway' and by no less an authority than W C Slingsby as 'a grim monolith', it nevertheless looked highly attractive to us and immediately became the next feature of the 'sports plan'.

The first problem was how to approach the peak, which has a remote location at the head of Stetfjord. The answer was to try to hire a boat. Next day, after a hot and rather tedious walk from Skardberget to Lysvoll with heavy packs, it proved surprisingly easy to arrange for a local fishing boat to take us about 12km to the head of the fjord. As we chugged up the fjord, with Stetind growing ever closer, we looked at the impossible terrain on either side and realized we had definitely made a good decision to approach by sea. (Nowadays there is a road.) That evening we pitched the tent on a patch of grass beside a stream near the shore and boiled up some fresh fish, kindly given to us by a local fisherman. Long after we lost the sun it continued to light the granitic slabs high above on Stetind.

The ordinary route leads round the back (south) of Stetind and over a subsidiary peak called Halls Foretopp, and then up the south ridge (Sydpillaren). This is the route which defeated a strong Alpine Club party consisting of Collie, W E and A M Slingsby in bad weather in 1904. It was first climbed by a Norwegian party the following year.

From our camp, a path led through a birch wood beside a stream and then gained height, passing over bilberry slopes until it reached a small lake at 700m. From the lake, the route led over easy scree to a col below Presttind. We were beginning to wonder if we would just walk to the top of Stetind when we reached the top of Hall's Foretopp and gained a view of the final ridge: the rope and gear would certainly be needed! The crux pitch was a very exposed but well protected hand-traverse, which we avoided by abseil on the descent. The summit was a flat, boulder area, about the size of a football pitch, a most un-summit-like summit. Needless to say, the views were marvellous.

After Stetind, I was naively concerned that Lofoten might be an anticlimax. I needn't have worried. The peaks are very different but no less spectacular. The crossing from Narvik to Svolvaer, in a jet boat weaving between rocky islands at 30 knots, with the silhouette of the mountains in the low sun, was one of the highlights of our holiday.

We found that the peaks in Lofoten were very steep and what looked like grass from a distance was a tangle of birch scrub, bilberry and ferns hiding ankle-breaking scree. The rock was coated in lichen and felt insecure and the topography was extremely complex. Our climbing was not very successful.

After a couple of failures, we managed to climb Geitgaljartind by the north-east ridge, repeating the route taken by Collie, Hasting and others in 1901.

Before leaving Lofoten, we climbed The Goat, a rock pinnacle situated seemingly vertically above the Svolvaer town cemetery. It made a pleasant change to climb on clean rock without a rucksack. The top consists of two horns and the lower horn is reached by an airy jump from the upper. Never keen on jumping, the look on my face, having made the leap, was enough to cause John to burst out in hysterical laughter.

We were lucky to have almost perfect weather, and very few mosquitoes, throughout our fortnight in Arctic Norway. It was a great pleasure to sit outside the tent by a campfire, watching the sunset each evening. On our final afternoon in Lofoten, the cloud base came right down and it started to rain, as if to show us what might have been, but by then we were already on the boat starting our long journey home.

John Evans climbing on Huglehornet.

Stetind.

Approaching Lofoten in evening.

Sixteen

Karakoram

John Evans, stark naked, was chasing a rat around our room with a ski stick. It wasn't a dream: we were staying at Flashman's Hotel, a traditional old hotel in Rawalpindi.

In 1987, together with two other London Mountaineering Club members, Gary Weston and Paul Allum, we had decided to visit the Karakoram. The Karakoram is a range of mountains spanning the borders of China, Pakistan and India, with the greatest concentration of high mountains in the world. From the beautiful Royal Geographical Society map surveyed by members of Eric Shipton's 1939 expedition, we chose, as our objective, a peak in the north of Pakistan, to the south-west of the Biafo Glacier.

From Islamabad, we took a flight to Skardu, with great views of Nanga Parbat, the ninth highest peak in the world, which has an isolated position south of the main Karakoram chain. Unfortunately, the pilot was not able to find a way down through the clouds and we flew back to Islamabad. The well-known Austrian mountaineer Kurt Diemberger, whose biography *Summits and Secrets* is one of the better mountaineering books, was in the same predicament. He was very friendly and helpful to a group of Karakoram novices but, in the end, we decided to charter our own minibus for the long journey up the Karakoram Highway.

Completed in 1986, and also known as the Friendship Highway, this road connects China and Pakistan and is a marvel of engineering, carving a line through the cliffs high above the River Indus. The road is constantly swept by landslides and rockfall but these are generally cleared quickly by the bulldozers of the Pakistan Army Corps of Engineers. We jolted and rattled northward, with the inevitable breakdowns. That night was spent at Besham, a dirty village where our evening meal, eaten with our hands, was probably responsible for the sickness which struck next day, at about the time we reached Gilgit.

The road on from Gilgit to Skardu was, if anything, even more spectacular.

The valley seemed deeper and the river was nearer, so we were more aware of its immense force. The geology was written into the bare rock faces. In the distance were snowy mountains and, wherever there was water, vivid green vegetation made a stunning contrast with the surrounding browns and greys. At the end, the valley opened out into a wide plain and we drove into Skardu.

We spent another poor night, in and out of the bathroom, at the K2 Motel. In the morning, with our sirdar, Shaban, we bought food such as sugar, rice and potatoes in the bazaar and, in the afternoon, we had a mass of chaotic packing to sort out. Next morning, seven tough-looking Balti porters turned up, the kit was loaded into a Toyota pick-up truck and, together with the porters, we piled on top for the drive up the Shigar Valley.

At the end of the road, we set off for the Braldu Gorge and camped after a couple of hours. Next day, we continued through the gorge, a very dry, barren valley. The path was dusty, the streams were muddy and the heat was intense. It seemed a hard country compared to Nepal. In the afternoon we crossed the thundering Braldu River in a rickety, old crate, suspended by a pulley below a single wire, and camped at Chongo.

We were refreshed by some hot springs the next morning, and an easier day's walk to Askole, the last village. It seemed very medieval. The houses were built from stone held together by mud, with wooden beams supporting a flat, mud roof. Through small, square windows we could see a few women sitting on the earth floors. The main irrigation channel flowed down the main street, providing drinking water, washing facilities and drainage.

A sharp turn north-west off the main Baltoro path the next day soon gave us our first view of the Biafo Glacier. As we walked up it in the afternoon, we had a great view of the spectacular Latok peaks and the Ogre. We camped in a sandy hollow beside the moraine and I cooked the evening meal on a wood fire. By the following day, continuing up the Biafo Glacier, partly on moraine and partly on dry ice, we were beginning to feel the altitude. When we reached our base camp at Ho Bluk the next day, a flowery, grassy moraine, we were rewarded with an unrivalled view of some of the world's most spectacular mountains. We paid off Shaban and the porters; it was quite poignant watching them leave.

Two days later, on Gary's birthday, we reached the summit of a small snow peak just over 6000m high. We spent a cold night bivouacking on the snow a few hundred metres lower and in the morning decided to descend to base camp. The glacier approach had been quite frightening and I think we were a bit overwhelmed by the remoteness of the situation. After a couple of days, we set off to trek up the glacier to Snow Lake. Sadly, I was feeling ill and returned to camp, where I rested and read my book, Eric Newby's *Love and War in the Apennines*. Two days, later the others returned, looking tired and thin.

On our departure day there was no sign of the porters so, leaving some gear on a large rock for collection later, we set off back to Askole. It took two days, descending to thicker air and warmer temperatures. Back in Askole, we collapsed in the shade of some trees and Shaban brought us some welcome chapattis and eggs.

The walk out seemed a lot more relaxing than the walk in. I was finally fit and acclimatized and I felt in a strange mood, less keen to return to civilization now the end was in sight. We got back to Skardu in a dust storm and, after two rather tense days, as we had already discovered the flights were unreliable, we departed by Boeing 737, passing so close to Nanga Parbat that we couldn't properly see all the mountain.

The Karakoram was a tough trip and we learnt a lot of lessons. We got ill and the walk in was harder than expected; then we had to cope with the altitude and, near the end, we ran out of food. I have not been back but, were I to go again, I would definitely employ a good cook. Only two weeks later, I was back in Pakistan, working in Sind Province where Lasmo was starting a seismic survey. Driving around the Indus Valley, making a reconnaissance of the area, was colourful, interesting and less stressful than the Karakoram.

Paul Allum crossing the Braldu River.

On the Biafo Glacier.

The summit of 'Birthday Peak.'

PART 3
The Far East

*He is lucky who, in the full tide of life, has experienced a measure
of the active environment he most desires.
In these days of upheaval and violent change, when the basic values
of to-day are the vain and shattered dreams of to-morrow,
there is much to be said for a philosophy which aims at
living a full life while the opportunity offers.
There are few treasures of more lasting worth than the experience
of a way of life that is in itself wholly satisfying.
Such, after all, are the only possessions of which no fate,
no cosmic catastrophe can deprive us;
nothing can alter the fact if for one moment
in eternity we have really lived.*

ERIC SHIPTON, IN **UPON THAT MOUNTAIN**, 1943

Photo opposite: Karst limestone scenery at Phang Nga in Thailand.

Seventeen

Malaysia
and Indonesia

Malaysia

Kuala Lumpur is Malaysia's fast-growing capital city. I was unexpectedly posted there in 1990, following Lasmo's take-over of a small Canadian company. Lasmo operated a concession off the north-east coast of the Malaysian peninsular and my job was to map the whole area in only a few months and identify three prospects (drillable structures) before the arrival of a rig. I enjoyed working in a small office, where I found more comradeship between colleagues than in London.

I lived in a comfortable flat in a small, well-designed development around a swimming pool, about 3km from the city centre. My lifestyle of climbing weekends was now over, but we did find some rock climbing on Bukit Takun, an impressive pinnacle of karst limestone a few kilometres north of the city, and some scrambling on Klang Gates, a quartzite ridge on the edge of the jungle to the west.

There was much to enjoy in Malaysia. I found the local people very cheerful and quick to smile. Malaysians are passionate about food and Kuala Lumpur has some of the best in the world, with superb Malaysian, Indian and Chinese cuisine available everywhere, from warungs (small street stalls) to five-star hotels. I soon made friends with other expatriates and at weekends we played tennis and visited different bars and restaurants.

I drove a Malaysian-made Proton car and enjoyed visiting and photographing villages, plantations, the jungle and the coast within range of Kuala Lumpur. The many Muslim, Chinese and Christian public holidays gave me a chance to explore further afield, using local flights, and I visited Penang, Langkawi, Phuket in Thailand and even Hong Kong. Langkawi was a favourite place.

It was fun to ride a hired moped around the island, with its beautiful jungle-clad hills, terraced paddy fields and tropical beaches. At the time, there was only one smart hotel, Langkawi Island Resort, and my family came to Malaysia for a memorable Christmas there.

Malaysia has one large mountain, Kinabalu (4105m) in Sabah, on the island of Borneo. Jay came out to visit in July 1991 and we flew to Kota Kinabalu with the objective of climbing the mountain. We took a beat-up old taxi directly from the airport to the Park Headquarters, grinding uphill into the Crocker Range, often in first gear, through extremely thick mist. Rain fell all afternoon. What with a bumpy flight, misty drive, wet afternoon and damp beds, morale was rather low the first night.

In the morning, the mist cleared for a short time to allow us a good view of the mountain, surprisingly close at hand. We took a (compulsory) guide and set off under an archway at the start of the trail. The path was well made and the ascent unremitting. Our guide, Richard, showed us some carnivorous pitcher plants. Slowly the taller trees gave way to a gnarled scrubby variety and shrubs. We had good views of the jungle-clad hills through gaps in the mist. After four and a half hours, we reached the Laban Rata Resthouse, at the foot of massive, granite slabs at 3200m. It was quite like an Alpine hut. There were a few other couples, mostly German, and a party of Koreans. For a while, the mountain was clear, with a sea of white clouds below, but then the mist rose, there was an afternoon storm and the rock slabs were soon streaming with torrents of water.

In the morning, we made an 'Alpine' start, rising at 2.30am and leaving an hour later. Bizarrely, the first 100m of trail was lit by streetlights. The path climbed steeply on a ladder of wooden branches and then traversed onto the granite slabs. We passed a small hut, Sayat-Sayat, and continued entirely over smooth rock, following a fixed rope. Gradually it got less dark, until head-torches were no longer necessary. Near the edge of Low's Gully, I scrambled to the edge to peer over into unfathomable depths.

A few minutes later, we reached the summit of Low's Peak. We sat just out of the wind, hoping for a clearance, but the mist persisted and after twenty minutes I noticed that Jay's teeth were chattering, so we returned to the hut. Luckily we had allowed two days and next morning we retraced the route in clear weather. Kinabalu is a large massif with several summits. Leaving the crowds on Low's Peak, we walked across to Victoria Peak and, while our guide Richard stayed at the bottom, we scrambled up steep, exposed granite rocks to the summit about 200m higher. There was a good view of almost the whole of Sabah in the early morning light. We didn't try to reach the very highest point, a large finger of rock leaning out over Low's Gully, as this requires about 20m of serious, unprotected rock climbing above a drop of several hundred metres.

147

In the afternoon, we descended all the way back to the Park Headquarters. It got harder and harder on the legs and, for the last few hundred metres, my thighs felt as if they were turning to jelly. At the bottom we were given a certificate for that day which read: '…attempted to climb Low's Peak 4105m and reached Victoria Peak 4094m'. Next day, while relaxing on the beach at Sapi Island, we could see Kinabalu dominating the view. We were both extremely stiff and we still joke about 'Kinabalu thighs'.

Indonesia

Soon after Jay's visit to Malaysia, my work there came to an end. Our third well made a large gas discovery, but at that time the market for gas was limited, and Lasmo sold their Malaysian interests to ExxonMobil. I was transferred to Indonesia. Jakarta, with its crowds, slums and traffic, seemed initially less pleasant than Kuala Lumpur, but outside the city Indonesia has much more variety and interest than Malaysia, with historical sites such as Borobudur and Prambanan, great beaches, tea plantations, terraced rice paddies, jungle and, of course, a chain of volcanoes.

I lived in a large house with a private swimming pool in the Kemang area of Jakarta, and I had four servants: a driver, maid, gardener and night guard. None of them spoke a word of English so I had to learn a little Bahasa fast. This proved to be a great benefit when travelling. The first few sentences of a conversation were often predictable, with an early question almost always being, *'Berapa anak anak ada?'* (How many children do you have?).

My first Indonesian volcano was Gunung Gede, the nearest to Jakarta, which I climbed with Alastair Hill, a colleague from Malaysia. It was pleasant to drive out of Jakarta, leaving behind the polluted air and the buses belching black smoke. At Bogor, on the edge of the hills, we stopped for some shopping in the colourful bazaar. I was struck by the method of carrying goods: everything was transported in two baskets or containers suspended from a wooden strip balanced on one shoulder.

We started our climb at 1.00 next morning, walking up the trail through the jungle by head-torch, taking care to avoid branches at head height. After about two hours we came to a hot stream, with steam rising into the air and a noticeable smell of sulphur; a strange place in the moonlight. The trees became smaller and the trail steepened. The locals wore thick clothing and balaclavas but it wasn't particularly cold. We reached the tree-line suddenly after about four hours and it wasn't far beyond to the edge of the crater. We followed the trail around the rim, arriving at the summit at about 5.30. There was a beautiful view of distant volcanoes away to the east. After about twenty minutes, the sun rose but I discovered I had lost my camera on the ascent, so it wasn't only the volcano that was fuming. It took about four hours to descend, with a short detour to some fine waterfalls.

Gunung Gede was typical of many Indonesian volcanoes, with a long, steep climb from about 1500m to about 3000m, usually done in the dark as the best chance of clear views is at dawn. I joined a club called the Java Lavas, run by an Austrian gentleman, which arranged a volcano trip about once a month. It was a great way to get to know Java. Typically, we would fly to somewhere like Jogjakarta on a Friday evening and climb the volcano early the next morning, then on the Sunday morning we would visit a local attraction such as a waterfall, temple or lake before an afternoon flight back to Jakarta.

Noteworthy trips included Semeru, the highest volcano in Java, which erupted with terrifying power every half-hour, and Bromo, rightly well known for its beautiful scenery. In general, the volcanoes are less forested and more interesting to visit, the further east one goes in Java. Jay came to visit me in Indonesia and we climbed Merapi with a local guide. There were a lot of sulphurous fumes on top. (In recent years Merapi has erupted violently with deadly effect.) Later the same week Jay and I went to Bali. Bali is stunningly beautiful and the place where our long friendship became a romance. Starting from a typical, attractive Balinese temple, we climbed Gunung Agung, the volcano dominating the north of the island. From the top, we had good views across to Gunung Rinjani on the island of Lombok.

Rinjani, which dominates Lombok, is an active volcano 3726m high. It required a four-day trek with colleagues from the office but was easily the best Indonesian volcano I climbed. The mountain consists of a recent volcanic cone inside a much bigger caldera with a lake. On the first day, we climbed from sea level to camp at about 2000m. Next day, we crossed the rim of the outer caldera, at about 2500m, and dropped down to camp by the beautiful lake. The third morning, we climbed to the summit. It was hard work at over 3500m on loose scree, but we were rewarded by a great sunrise. On the final day we trekked back out to the coast. I have very happy memories of that trip – although it was a big mistake to try to get my photographs developed locally, for the shop managed to mangle two out of four films. Despite this hiccup, I thought Lombok a delightful island and a highlight of my three years in the Far East.

Bukit Takun. Karst limestone near Kuala Lumpur.

A view to Victoria Peak from Low's Peak on Kinabalu. *Photo: J. Turner.*

Gunung Agung on Bali seen from Lombok.

The summit of Gunung Rinjani.

Gunung Rinjani, the most beautiful of all the volcanoes in Indonesia.

EIGHTEEN

Japan

Eighty-five percent of Japan is mountainous. The highest peaks, apart from the volcanic cone of Mount Fuji (3776m), lie in the centre of Honshu Province, only about 200km north-west of Tokyo, where the most northerly of three mountain ranges has been designated the Chubu-Sangaku (Japan Alps) National Park.

The idea of climbing in Japan came from my friend Mark Lowe, who was living in Hong Kong, and we arranged a visit in July 1991. The city of Matsumoto acts as a gateway to the Chubu-Sangaku National Park and we arrived there at about midnight, having taken an express train from Tokyo's Shinjuku station. After some difficulty, we found a room in a nearby hotel. The door was about 5ft 7in high, a sensible height for me but not for Mark who is nearly 6ft tall. The interior was small, with the bedding lying directly on the tatami-matted floor, and with beautiful, wafer thin papering on the cupboard doors. Rucksacks and climbing boots do not mix well with Japanese rooms.

Matsumoto is famous for its castle, which has a five-tiered donjon built in the sixteenth century. From the castle, there is a fine view of the distant mountains. The remainder of the city, like most Japanese towns, was clean and modern but lacking in any beauty. Above all the streets there was a forest of electric wires and advertising signs. Having inspected the castle and town, we took a private railway to Shimashima and then a crowded bus, which climbed through wooded hills and passed through several tunnels to reach the road-head at Kamicochi. It is located in the Azusa River valley at an altitude of 1500m, with the mountains all around. Here there are hotels, gift shops and a campsite, where we pitched our tent.

Kamicochi is a popular local destination and the Kappa Bridge, a suspension bridge over the crystal clear waters of the Azusa River, is always thronged with tourists. About twenty minutes walk downstream, there is a memorial to the Reverend Walter Weston, an Alpine Club member who climbed Yari Ga-Dake and other peaks of the Hotaka mountains between 1888 and1894. The term

'Japanese Alps' was popularized by his celebrated book *Mountaineering and Exploring in the Japanese Alps.*

We awoke to the sound of steady rain on the tent. After a long and tiring journey, I was quite relieved by the excuse for a lie-in. Fortunately, at about 9.00, Mark looked out and saw that the water level was rising steadily around the tent. We fled to a cafe. It took most of the rest of the week to dry out the soggy pages of my passport and airline tickets but, even in the rain, the valley around Kamicochi, with its mossy pine, larch and silver-birch woods, marshy areas and clear streams, had an exquisite beauty. It was easy to see the inspiration for much of Japanese art.

The next day dawned sunny, with steam rising from the cold water of the river. We soon dried out the worst of our wet clothes and set off with sleeping bags, bivvy bags, stove and food for four days. The objective was a traverse of the main Japanese Alps from Yari Ga-Dake (3180m) to Maehotaka-Dake (3090m). This route is one of the most popular mountain trips in Japan and is equipped with several huts but, as they can be crowded and are invariably expensive, we chose to be independent.

We followed the wide valley bottom with its stony riverbed for several hours, then climbed steeply through the forest beside an attractive torrent. Above were grassy slopes with a mass of wildflowers. The mountains and valley reminded me strongly of the Pyrenees. When, after walking for about eight hours, we reached a splendid bivouac spot with shelter, water and a fine view over the ridges to the distant cone of Mount Fuji, I was all for stopping. Mark, however, persuaded me to continue, since the shapely rock peak of Yari Ga-Dake was only about another hour away. It was lucky that he did, as the peak was lost in mist all the next day. We climbed over scree for about half an hour to reach the ridge, where we left our packs at a large hut. A further half-hour of scrambling took us to the summit. It was a beautiful viewpoint with lovely mist effects, including a Brocken spectre, in the evening light. We had to bivouac near the hut, in order to buy water, but unfortunately our site (on a ridge at over 3000m) was quite exposed. The wind increased steadily until the violent flapping of the bivvy bags in the middle of the night forced us inside the hut to seek shelter.

For the next three days we traversed along the ridge over several 3000m summits. Some of the time we were in thick mist and could easily have been on a ridge in Scotland; at other times the cloud would suddenly blow away to reveal deep, wooded valleys below. Parts of the route had enjoyable scrambling but the more technical sections were all equipped with chains or ladders. We both felt slightly irritated by the abundance of paint marks and ladders but, on the last day in wild wind and driving rain, we could understand their necessity on such a popular route.

The huts were not unlike Swiss huts, except for the dining room. Here, one evening, we sat cross-legged on a matted floor, eating with chopsticks from a table only a few inches high. The bulk of the meal consisted of seaweed and sticky white rice; the cost of a night, plus evening meal, was 7,000 yen (about £35).

The traverse of the main ridge completed our primary objective and we planned to do some rock climbing. Unfortunately, the next day we again had heavy rain. (Apparently June and July are the rainy season in the Japanese Alps and prospective visitors would do better to choose August or September.) Camping below the dripping trees brought back indelible memories of my first Alpine season, camping in the woods at Argentière.

Although there is some rock climbing on high crags near the ridge, the best is on Byobu Rock, a large granite crag about 15km up the valley from Kamicochi. Mark had obtained some topo route descriptions by writing to a Japanese climber he had met on a previous visit to Japan.

Next morning, we set out in cloudy weather. The approach to Byobo Rock took three and a half hours and included a knee-deep wade across an icy river. We scrambled up a long boulder gully to a large snow patch; from there, three pitches of V Diff climbing, followed by some scrambling, led to a terrace where the routes start. All the climbs on Byobo Rock were artificial, mostly graded IV/A1 or V/A2. Pegs and bolts littered the rock, even where natural protection was available. The crag is several hundred metres high and, with the mist drifting in and out, looked black, wet and daunting. After a few minutes, the heavens opened and there was torrential rain. We abseiled down, water pouring through our sleeves, and made our sodden way back to the Kamicochi campsite.

Next morning – brilliantly sunny at last, with the valley at its most beautiful – we had to leave for Tokyo.

Mark Lowe on Yari Ga-Dake.

NINETEEN

New Zealand

'Heavy traffic today,' said Frances Price as we drove south from Christchurch on New Zealand's Route 1. I looked around in astonishment; a single car was visible about half a mile ahead and another vehicle had passed in the opposite direction a few minutes earlier. To the west, about 45km away, we could clearly see the snow-clad mountains of the Southern Alps. Having just flown in from Jakarta, one of the most crowded and polluted cities in the world, with constant traffic jams and a population four times bigger than the whole of New Zealand, I was in a state of culture shock.

Frances and her New Zealand husband Dick were hosts to me and four Eagle Ski Club members who had flown directly from England: Mike Daly, Geoff Timms, Charlotte Turner (Jay's sister) and Jos Widdereshoven. We were guided by Geoff Wyatt. Dick was an experienced Himalayan climber, who soon became affectionately known as 'Burra-sah'b'. With no allowance for jet jag, we drove all the way to Twizel on the day of arrival, as the forecast was favourable for flying to the Tasman Glacier the following day. Twizel, originally a hydroelectric town, lies about 8km south of Mount Cook village.

Cloud prevented glacier flights next morning, so in the afternoon we made a short ski-tour to a small peak above the local ski resort of Lake Ohau. From the top we had a fine view of snowy peaks lit by the evening sun, reflected in the still waters of the lake. For some of us, it was the first time on skis for over a year and the descent, over difficult crusty snow, was punctuated by a series of craters.

Next morning, we made an early start and drove to the airport at Mount Cook. Food was crammed into bulging rucksacks, we were bundled into two light aircraft and, with a noticeable lack of pre-flight checks, off we went. We flew over the wide gravels below the Tasman Glacier and climbed through a small bank of mist to emerge to a dramatic view of the massive east face of Mount Cook, dazzling white in the sunlight. Minutes later we were standing in powdery snow high on the Tasman Glacier. It was perfect weather but the temperature of -10°C was quite a shock after the 30°C in Jakarta. The departing plane left tiny snow crystals glinting in the sunlight.

We spent four days on the Tasman Glacier, all in fine weather. For the first two nights we were based at the Kelman Hut, which is perched on a ridge above the Tasman Saddle. On the first day we climbed a narrow snow arête leading to Hochstetter Dome, which made an exciting start. Next day, after some crevasse rescue training in a real crevasse, we climbed Mount Aylmer, again roping up for a final narrow snow arête. From the top, we had a wonderful view northwards along the Southern Alps, with a sea of sharp, pointed peaks lit by the evening sun.

The third day, we schussed down the glacier with heavy packs and made an interesting side excursion up the Darwin Glacier, where the steep rock and ice walls brought back memories of Greenland. After spending the night in the Beetham Hut, situated in a side valley below the impressive face of Malte Brun, we skied down the glacier, climbed a horrendous moraine about 50m high to the site of the old Ball Hut and made our way on skis and then on foot out to the car.

Driving round to the west coast over the next two days, we marvelled at the contrast between the dry, desert-like scenery on the east side of the divide and the dense, temperate rainforest on the west. From Fox Village, we helicoptered to the Pioneer Hut. The use of aircraft and helicopters is widespread and highly practical in New Zealand; it enabled us to maximize the fun of skiing and climbing, and minimize load-carrying with heavy sacks. It also had the advantage of allowing a very much higher standard of catering in the huts than the awful freeze-dried meals I remembered from the Pyrenees.

It is hard to know which was the highlight of our time on the Fox Glacier. Perhaps an ascent of Mount Grey in a surprising clearance after a day of snow, with lovely powder snow on the descent; or a wondrous west coast sunset later that evening; or the ascent of an extremely spectacular arête onto Mount Lendenfeld from Marcel Col the next day. We skied down to the Chancellor Hut and helicoptered out to the coast just as bad weather came in from the west.

Our final few days in the mountains were spent in the Mount Aspiring National Park. Again, we used a helicopter to gain access to the Bonar Glacier below Mount Aspiring. One minute we were waiting for the helicopter on a spring-like day in the valley, then, only minutes later, we were in a completely different, dazzling white world on the 'quarterdeck' at over 2000m. The Colin Todd Memorial Hut provided a cosy base for the next two nights, once we had emptied it of large volumes of snow. Cosy it certainly was: there was only room for three to stand at one time.

In the morning, Dick and I formed a splinter group to climb Mount Aspiring by the Ramp and north-west ridge. We enjoyed a perfect winter's day without a breath of wind. The summit was a beautiful, triangular snow cone and we could see Mount Cook over 150km away. Two days later we clambered down through the tangled bush of French Ridge to Geoff Wyatt's own hut at Shovel Flat. The sheltered, mossy forest made a striking contrast with the snows above. Next day, we walked for a few hours down the broad Matukituki Valley until we reached the cars.

Our last days were devoted to being tourists. A day's visit to Coronet Peak reminded me of everything I dislike about piste-skiing: muddy car parks, crowds and ugly lifts. A visit to Milford Sound was much more rewarding, for the Fjordland scenery was fabulous, with steep-sided, snowy peaks towering above the bush. Equally memorable was the wildlife: leaping dolphins played about our jet boat and seals sunned themselves on the shoreline rocks.

On the last night of this holiday, one of the best winter holidays I have ever had, Geoff Wyatt made a short speech. 'Don't ever, ever, come back,' he said, 'because you will never have it so good again!'

Ski plane on the Tasman Glacier.

Ski-touring high on the Tasman Glacier.

West coast sunset, on the Fox Glacier.

Descending Mount Lendenfeld.

Dick Price near the top of Mount Aspiring, a beautiful summit.

On a small rock pinnacle near Mount Aspiring with a view to the west. *Photo: G. Wyatt.*

PART 4
Recent Highlights

Ultimately and most importantly,
mountains quicken our sense of wonder…
Mountains return to us the priceless capacity for wonder which
can so insensibly be leached away by modern existence,
and they urge us to apply that wonder
to our everyday lives.

ROBERT MACFARLANE, IN **MOUNTAINS OF THE MIND**, 2003

Photo opposite: A Scots Pine in Glen Quoich.

TWENTY

Aonach Mor

I was made redundant by Lasmo in 1993, one of the many downturn periods in the oil industry. I returned to Britain from the Far East and, needing somewhere to live, I made a spur-of-the-moment decision to rent an old farmhouse in the village of Pegsdon, immediately below the Chiltern Hills in Bedfordshire. Bury Farm dated from the seventeenth century and, although it was cold in winter, with no central heating, I never regretted my decision. I lived there for nearly three years before I found a permanent job with Geco-Prakla (now WesternGeco) and I enjoyed learning about gardening, growing flowers and vegetables, and watching the changing seasons in the countryside. It was in the garden at Bury Farm that I finally proposed to Jay on a fine evening in early summer. Luckily she said 'yes' without needing to consider the answer for too long and that year we spent many pleasurable weekends visiting old haunts in the Peak District, Exmoor, North Wales and the Lake District. We also spent a week in Italy, climbing in the Gran Paradiso area, as described in an earlier chapter.

I had now been climbing mountains for twenty years without any accidents. I had twice had battles with high winds, in the Cairngorms and in Greenland, and I had encountered tragedy near the CIC Hut on Ben Nevis when two climbers fell from Tower Ridge, but I had not suffered any misfortune myself. That was to change in Scotland in the winter of 1994.

I set out with two friends from the London Mountaineering Club to climb the North-East Ridge of Aonach Beag. To reach the climb, we used the ski lifts at Aonach Mor and, from a small hut at the top of the lift system, walked towards the summit of the mountain. It was cloudy, with snow underfoot, conditions known as 'white-out'. I went in front, having taken a careful compass-bearing.

After only a few hundred metres I was suddenly falling. I realized instantly that I must have walked onto a cornice but it was too late to do anything. I fell, vertically, past rocks and then slid on and on down steep snow before slowly coming to a halt. I was alive! Slowly I gathered my wits. My breeches were around my ankles, I had lost my gloves and there was some blood on the snow but I seemed to be intact. I stood up and my right leg bent forward at a funny angle. I sat down, feeling sick, and then stood up a lot more carefully and, leaning on my axe, started to hobble slowly down. I blew my emergency whistle for the first time ever when I saw some climbers below.

Meanwhile, one of my friends had gone for help at the ski station while the other started to construct a belay so that they could look over the edge of the cornice. Before he had finished, a piste-bashing machine rumbled up and the driver said, 'Better to tie the rope here.' Naturally, there was no sign of me just below. One of the pisteurs skied down Easy Gully and found me just after a pair of climbers from Swansea had come to my assistance. They supported me between their shoulders as we made our way slowly round the hillside, until a piste-basher took me back to the ski rescue station. It was there that I learnt from the ski patrol team that the Ordnance Survey map had marked the top ski lift in the wrong location. The map was based on original plans and showed the top lift 200m away from the edge of the corrie. In fact, it was built very close to the rim.

It transpired that I had severed the anterior cruciate ligament in my right knee and I required arthroscopic surgery. Of course, I was very lucky not to have been killed, having fallen vertically for about 75m and then about 200m down snow slopes. I thought long and hard about suing the Ordnance Survey but decided it was better to focus on finding a job. The incident received some publicity on Scottish television and in the Daily Telegraph, under the headline 'The man who was nearly killed by his map'.

I recovered steadily from the surgery without needing to have the cruciate ligament rebuilt. By the autumn I was walking and climbing again and, the following spring, Jay and I joined an unguided Eagle Ski Club party in the Gran Paradiso area. I carried an extremely light rucksack and wore a small neoprene brace on my knee.

Jay and I were married on a perfect spring day in 1996. We spent our honeymoon walking and relaxing in Crete. The island was carpeted with wildflowers and there was still snow on the White Mountains. It was an ideal honeymoon choice.

TWENTY ONE

Mallorca and Spain

My first visit to Mallorca was at Christmas 1995 and I quickly fell under its charm. I loved the climate, after the cold of mid-winter in Britain, the attractive old villages with their mellow stone, the orange trees and the fine farmhouses amid the olive groves. Jay's family had rented an apartment on the Pine Walk at Port de Pollença, with a marvellous view across the bay to the Alcudia Peninsular. The summits of Tomir and Puig Roig were visible behind the modern buildings of the town. We returned there for Christmas in 1997.

Jay's family were already familiar with much of the walking in the Sierra de Tramuntana and were avid readers of June Parker's guidebook to the island. The walking is very varied and the limestone rock gives some excellent scrambling. We had some good days above the steep coastal cliffs near Cala de san Vicenç and on the Formentor Peninsular. One of the highlights was climbing the Cavall Bernat Ridge, which plunges vertically into the sea on one side. Other good days included ascents of Puig Gros de Ternelles and Puig Roig. Also memorable was a fine walk to Rafal d'Ariant, a remote ruined farmhouse near the coast, with Jay's elderly father.

Over the following years, Jay and I returned to Mallorca several times, staying in different parts of the island, including Sant Elm and Port de Soller. Our most recent visit was in 2007, staying near Alcudia with our friends Ken White and Alison Graham, and Mike and Valerie Hendry. We have climbed all the main mountains, such as Masanalla and Puig de Galatzó, incorporating scrambles whenever possible. Ronnie Watham, at the Alpine Club, told us about a secret path up the steep cliffs above Deià, a fine way to the summit of Teix, which we have done twice. Sadly, access problems in Mallorca seem to be worsening and some of the best walks are now barred with impassable fences.

As well as Mallorca, we have visited several other mountain areas in Spain at New Year, including the limestone mountains inland from the Costa Blanca and the Sierra de Serella, which we explored from the attractive village of Quatretondetta. Another visit was to the Alpujarras, where we followed ancient Mozarabic trails between the flat-roofed Moorish villages below the snowy peaks of the Sierra Nevada.

Our second favourite place for winter walking is the Sierra Grazelema in Andalucia, where we twice rented rooms at Montecorto from Guy Hunter-Watts, who wrote the local guide book. From the nearby summit of Lagarin, we watched the majestic griffon vultures circling the ridge very close to us, and we walked through the famous Pinsapo pine trees and climbed to the highest summit, Pinar (El Torreon) at 1654m. An alternative attraction – and a delight to explore – were the Andalusian villages such as Grazelema, with narrow streets and tight-packed white buildings. And, of course, we enjoyed the Spanish food and wine.

We continued to travel to Spain at New Year with Ken and Alison until very recently. In 2006, we visited the Sierra Cazorla, which lies about 100km north-east of Granada. The weather was mixed and we spent two wet days looking at Renaissance palaces and churches in the nearby towns of Úbeda and Baeza, but we also had a fine day climbing Gilillo (1846m).

In 2008, we visited the Sierra Subbética, a range in the southern part of Cordoba province. We started in the mountain town of Zuheros, a typical *pueblo blanco* with tightly clustered white houses and a castle. The best walking was further south in the range, where we had excellent days on Pico Bermejo (1474m) and La Tiñosa (1568m). The mountains of both the Cazorla and Subbética are surrounded by mile upon mile of olive groves.

Our most recent winter visit to Spain was in 2009, when we stayed at Nerja on the Andalucian coast. Though the trip was spoiled by poor weather and illness, we managed an outstanding day on Tajo Almendrón (1514m). This dramatic limestone peak in the Sierra de Tejera is only a few kilometres inland from the Mediterranean coast. We spent another good day near Competa, north-east of Nerja. Jay is very skilled at finding maps and guidebooks for all our Spanish trips and we have never been disappointed by the walking, the scenery or the interesting towns and villages.

Jay on the Cavall Bernat Ridge.

Charlotte Turner, Jay's sister, on Puig Roig.

A typical Mallorcan farmhouse and olive grove.

Grazelema, with Pico San Cristóbal behind.

Twenty Two

Iran

Iran is more than three times the size of France and about half the country is covered by mountains. The Alborz range forms a great arc around the southern rim of the Caspian Sea and contains about seventy peaks over 4000m high, including Mount Damāvand (5671m), Iran's highest mountain. The Zagros mountains cover an even larger area on the west side of the country and consist of several north-west-trending mountain ranges parallel to the Gulf coast and Iran's border with Iraq. This is a wild area with several 4000m peaks and few roads.

The Alpine Ski Club expedition to these mountains was conceived, organized and led by David Hamilton. Including David, there were seventeen of us, with ages ranging from 26 to 63. David's plan, drawn up in conjunction with our local agent, Araz Adventure Tours, was to spend a few days in the Zagros, a few days in the Alborz near Shemshak ski resort and, finally, a few days attempting Mount Damāvand.

We flew overnight to Tehran via Istanbul with Turkish Airlines and on to Esfahan in the morning. Esfahan is home to some of the most majestic buildings in the Islamic world and later that morning, despite feeling tired and jet-lagged, we marvelled at the blue-tiled mosaic designs of the impressive Emām Mosque and the delicacy and lighting of the Sheikh Lotfollāh Mosque. Both mosques are located in the Emām Khomeinī Square and date from the Safavid Dynasty in the early seventeenth century. After a fine lunch, we also explored some of Esfahan's old bridges across the Zāyandeh River, inspected the eleventh-century Jāmeh Mosque and even found time for some tourist shopping. We were surprised at the wide range of western goods in the shops; David Beckham posters were obviously a bestseller.

Next morning, we travelled west by bus across rocky desert country towards the Zagros Mountains. The weather was poor, the countryside bleak and desolate and it started to rain and then to sleet as we neared our destination, a small road-head village called Chel Gerd below the Zard Kuh Range. We could just see a couple of Poma lifts on a snowy hillside as we offloaded our gear into a large brick building which appeared to be the village sports centre. We had the use of a sixteen-bunk dormitory room and the volleyball court in the next room. Meals were taken on the floor of the dormitory. In the afternoon, most of the party took the opportunity to ski in the mist and wet snow and discover the unique nature of the cloying, orange, Zagros mud.

The following day was much brighter but windy and fourteen of us set out for a hut at about 3400m in order to attempt Chal Mishan (4220m). We crossed the 2800m ridge behind our base, and descended on ski and foot to a valley and small dam at about 2400m on the far side. Then, a long way ahead of our porters, who were on foot and carrying stoves and food, we skinned up a long valley to a col and open slopes above. It became extremely windy as we neared the top of the slope, probably only a short distance below the hut. Due to slabby snow and zero visibility in the spindrift, we decided to retreat.

The party was spaced out, some still taking off skins, when there was a windslab avalanche. The spindrift limited my view of events but three members of the party were caught in the avalanche and one was carried a considerable distance. A separate avalanche buried two others, who were further down the slope, up to their waists. By good fortune, no one was completely buried and a chastened party reassembled at the col where the damage was assessed: lost gloves, poles and one lost ski.

We retraced our route of ascent. Some of the party climbed back up 400m to ski down to our base by head-torch, while others and the porters made a comfortable bivouac by breaking into a building near the dam. At a post-mortem the following afternoon, it was agreed, firstly, that we should have been more careful in assessing snow conditions on what was obviously a lee slope; and, secondly, that the size of the party made post-avalanche organization extremely difficult. We decided to keep more rigidly to smaller groups in future.

That night our building was struck by some astonishing gusts of wind, which brought masonry and dust falling from the ceiling. By morning, it was snowing steadily and we decided to leave the Zagros a day earlier than planned and travel by bus to Tehran and the Alborz Mountains. This decision was made with some regret, as the Zagros would undoubtedly provide fine ski-mountaineering in good weather. As we left the mountains, near Shahr Kord, the sun appeared and we had fine views of the almond trees in blossom, with snow-capped desert ranges in the background. It was a long drive to Tehran but I was captivated by the beautiful orange and pink colours of the desert rocks in the evening light.

After a night in Tehran's luxurious Evin Hotel, we travelled by bus to

Shemshak, a small ski resort about 30km north of Tehran, and installed ourselves in a comfortable hotel near one of the chairlifts. Following an afternoon of snow, we woke the next morning to sun at last, and several inches of fresh powder. For the first couple of hours we had the resort almost to ourselves for some wonderful off-piste skiing. Phil Ingle, who lives in the French Alps and skis every day, was able to demonstrate his prowess, including one astonishing jump over a cliff about 10m high. Several of us made an enjoyable half-day tour to a small ski peak, giving a good view of Mount Damāvand to the east, with its distinctive volcanic shape.

The next day was Ashūra, the anniversary of the martyrdom of Hossein, when Shiite Muslims mourn by whipping themselves with chains. Twelve of us, together with two local 'guides', headed off to a hut at 3575m, escaping the noise from the loudspeakers at the mosque. This time our ascent, although strenuous, was uneventful (the hardest part was climbing over a high metal fence while still in the town!) The hut was bare inside and we only just fitted in.

During the night it was windy, but the wind died down at dawn and we climbed the easy-angled ridge behind the hut on foot, some carrying skis. The ridge led to the summit of Colom Bassk (c 4100m). Most of us continued, some on foot and some on ski, along a pleasant ridge and over an intermediate lump, to the higher peak of Salak Chal (c 4220m), where we had a good view of Mount Damāvand to the east and the Alborz mountains all around. We were back at the hut by early afternoon after an excellent mountaineering day. In the distance we could see the remaining members of the party reaching the summit of a fine ski peak on a day tour from Shemshak.

Two days later we again loaded our gear onto a bus for the final phase of our trip, to Mount Damāvand. We joined a very busy road heading east from Tehran before turning north to the Caspian coast and the amazingly barren southern flanks of the Alborz mountains. The road climbed to a high pass at about 2700m, then dropped down the far side to a village called Polūr below the cloud-capped Mount Damāvand. There was a horrible smell of burning rubber from the rear wheel of our bus, so we had lunch in a restaurant while repairs were made. Fresh trout on the menu provided variety to the usual chicken or lamb kebabs. We drove on through rough volcanic terrain, with impressive views of the snowy north side of the Kūh-e Qarah Dāgh range. At the turn-off for the mountain, we piled into three Land Rovers, which gained us another 500m height up rough tracks. Finally, where the track was blocked by snow, mules were waiting to carry our skis to Gusfand Sara, at c 3150m, only a short distance away. A hut and adjacent mosque both offered dirty concrete floors; we chose the hut as some Iranians and Germans were already occupying the mosque.

Next morning, the mountain remained shrouded in cloud but thirteen of us continued, mostly on skis, up to the higher hut, Barghah-é-Sevvom, at 4150m. It was a small building with a semi-circular roof. Our relief at reaching this haven soon evaporated on finding utter bedlam, with Spanish, Iranian, German and Austrian parties all jostling for space in the dark interior. A patch of wet floor for our thermarests was the best most of us could manage and the afternoon passed playing a long game of Botticelli while a storm raged outside.

Despite wind all night, it was bright in the morning but, at over 4000m, extremely cold in the strong wind. Five hardy members decided to attempt the peak, while the others skied down to the lower hut on difficult, windblown snow. With binoculars and the two-hourly radio schedules, we could follow the progress of the summit party. Dave Wynne-Jones and John Kentish turned back during the morning, leaving David Hamilton, Alex Miller and Phil Ingle going strongly for the top. Sadly, but sensibly, Phil turned back at about 5000m with cold feet. David and Alex reached the summit at about 3.00pm, a terrific effort in the extreme conditions (estimated 75mph winds and a temperature of -26°C). They brought back reports of fumaroles, yellow sulphur rocks and a goat's head on the summit.

By 8.00pm the summit team had rejoined the rest of us at the restaurant in Polūr and before midnight we were back in the hotel in Tehran, a million miles from the squalor of the previous night. We had two days to sample the museums, palaces and restaurants of Tehran and, on the final night, we enjoyed a splendid meal provided at the home of one of our hosts at Araz Adventure Tours.

In common with many of us, I went to Iran with some apprehension following President Bush's 'axis-of-evil' speech. We found a more Western and more efficient country than expected. There was no problem with the authorities, the people we met were courteous and friendly, and our hosts from Araz Adventure Tours were charming and made great efforts to accommodate our every wish. We returned enriched by a greater appreciation of Persian history, art and culture, and with indelible memories of Iran's wonderful desert and mountain landscapes.

Alborz mountains near Shemshak.

Phil Ingle with Mount Damāvand in the background.

Twenty Three

Greece

Nearly all of the Greek peninsular is mountainous. When we went there in June 2005, with our friends Ken and Alison, we started in the Pindos Mountains in the north-west of the country. Jay and I arrived from Athens by hire car, crossing the new bridge over the Gulf of Corinth, and spent the first two nights at Tsepelovo, a rustic Zagorian village of stone-built houses with thick slate roofs, near the southern edge of the Vikos-Aoos National Park.

The Pindos are limestone mountains and it was obvious from our first day's walk up an ancient, stepped path, from Vadreto to the Beloi viewpoint over the deep Vikos Gorge, that the flora was exceptional. Compared to the Alps, the Pindos are unspoiled, with dense pine and beech forests on their lower slopes. We saw several tortoises (*testudo marginata*) which are common, and sometimes we moved them off roads. The region has several beautiful old packhorse bridges and we visited two near Kipi on the first afternoon.

Next day, from Vadreto, we followed a little-used path down into the Vikos Gorge. At the bottom, after stopping for a swim, we took the trail down the gorge. It is about 10km long and about 1000m deep, with densely vegetated walls of limestone on each side. In the hot afternoon sun we walked up to the attractive village of Papingo, situated on a terrace below limestone cliffs.

In the morning, we took the trail towards the Astraka Mountain Refuge, branching off on a small path to the south to traverse over the summit of Astraka (2436m). The flowers were quite exceptional; there were crocuses, lilies, daisies, forget-me-nots, gentians, wild tulips, orchids and many other varieties. We made our way down and round to the hut, which was situated above a lake and below the towering cliffs of Astraka. The hut had a guardian, who brought up supplies on horseback, but inside it was Spartan and slightly damp.

Gamila (2497m) is the highest point of the Timfi Range and we climbed it next day. It has huge cliffs plunging north towards the Aoos River. Once again, the flowers were superb and included small wild narcissi (*narcissus poeticus*) in the grykes of the limestone rock. We returned to the hut in a thunderstorm and, the following day, had an interesting walk through wild limestone country back to Tsepolovo. We tried to steer well clear of the shepherds' camps, which were guarded by very fierce dogs.

We then drove round to the north side of the Pindos to climb Smolikas (2637m), the second highest mountain in Greece. A stop was made near Konitsa, at the mouth of the Aoos River, to photograph another superb packhorse bridge. From the small village of Palioseli, it was possible to drive up a dirt track, zigzagging through the wooded hillside almost all the way to the small Smolikas Hut. The mountain is formed from serpentine rock, so it has a very different character to the limestone peaks to the south, with dense pine forests up to 2100m. Although rare, bears and wolves still roam these forests. Clouds spoiled the views from the summit next day, but Alison and Jay enjoyed identifying and photographing new species of orchids, lilies and other flowers.

After Smolikas, we parted from Ken and Alison, who had planned a longer holiday. Jay and I visited the extraordinary monasteries at Meteora, perched on top of inaccessible pinnacles of comglomerate rock. We then drove across to Litochoro, a pleasant town near the east coast, in order to climb Mount Olympus, the highest mountain in Greece.

From the road-head, we walked through pine woods to the Spílios Agapitós Hut, commonly known as Refuge A, at 2100m. Mount Olympus is a large massif, with several summits, and we had a good view from the hut. Frustratingly, though, the next day the weather was cloudy. We scrambled to the highest peak, Mitikas (2917m) but the cloud stubbornly refused to lift. To rub salt into the wound, the following day, from Litochoro, we could see the summits were clear again, but we had to return to Athens for our flight home.

Astraka.

Packhorse bridge near Kipi.

Flowers of the Pindos:

Leopard's Bane;

Wild Tulip;

Spring Gentian;

Poet's Narcissus;

Star of Bethlehem;

Forget-Me-Not.

TWENTY FOUR

Alpine Summits
and Flowers

I like all mountains but my favourite range is the Alps. The glaciers and snowfields add an extra dimension. Well-made paths and a network of huts provide access to the climbs, which can usually be completed in a day, and in early summer the dazzling displays of wildflowers in the meadows and on the upper rocky slopes greatly enhance the beauty of the surroundings.

Over the last twenty years, Jay and I have visited the Alps most summers. I gradually learnt that the higher summits are more enjoyable after becoming acclimatized to the altitude, so we tended to walk and climb on lower mountains before tackling 4000m peaks. In 1997, for example, we spent a few days traversing the Wildhorn, the Plein Morte Glacier and the Wildstrubel in the western Oberland, before moving to Saas Fee and climbing the Strahlhorn and Rimpfischhorn. We finished that season by climbing the Blümisaplhorn above the beautiful Oeschinensee lake near Kandersteg.

Similarly, in 1999, we spent a week traversing the valleys on the north side of the Val d'Aosta before going up to the Mantova Hut, above Alagna. From there, we climbed up to Monte Rosa, passing a pair of young British climbers who were suffering badly from the altitude, and we spent an excellent day visiting six of the different summits.

In the last ten years, in common with other mountaineers, some general wear developed in both Jay's knees and this resulted in less agility than in younger days. Jay is now slower descending mountains where there are loose rocks or awkward steps down, so we have therefore gradually reduced our mountaineering aspirations. At the same time, she has pursued a long-standing interest in Alpine flowers and diligently identifies and lists all the species we find, using the Collins pocket guide *Alpine Flowers of Britain and Europe* and any locally available regional flower books. Some of her enthusiasm has rubbed off on me. Just as I find a knowledge of geology enhances a day in the mountains, so I enjoy recognising the commoner flowers and, perhaps, spotting a rare orchid or a variety we have not yet seen. This growing awareness added greatly to the pleasure of the following two holidays, both in the Italian Alps and both particularly rewarding.

Brenta Dolomites

The Brenta Group is a range of rock summits about 3000m high, with towers, spires and dramatic, orange cliffs. Extending northwards from Lake Garda, and separate from the main Dolomites, it is famous for the Sentiero delle Bochette. This is a high-level via ferrata path, equipped with ladders and wire ropes, which connects horizontal ledges weaving a route through the heart of the range. It was constructed by members of the Società degli Alpinisti Trentini in the 1930s. The Brenta Dolomites are also famous for rare Alpine flora and the area is very popular with walkers and climbers. Jay and I wanted to try via ferrate and we visited in September 2004, right at the end of the summer season.

We started our holiday at Molveno, an attractive town beside a pleasant lake, with the spiky profile of the mountains visible above. Next morning, we took an antique lift (which involved running and jumping into a metal cage) and rose steeply through the trees as the roofs of Malveno receded below. It was quite misty as we walked up through the pine and beech woods, and the crags above, towards the Pedrotti Hut. My pack felt heavy but we admired the gentians and globe flowers, and a distinctive new flower which we identified at the hut as the rare Devil's Claw. My pack lightened considerably when the mist cleared!

Waking to a beautiful morning with a sea of cloud below, we followed a path south, contouring around the cirque. The views of the pale dolomite mountain cliffs all around were terrific and there was an amazing silence which made us feel like talking in whispers. After lunch on the terrace of the Agostini Hut, we continued, ascending a path above the hut until we reached the bottom of a long series of ladders disappearing up a vertical cliff into the mist. It looked very intimidating. However, we soon got into the rhythm, stopping every three metres to hook an elbow or arm over the rung while changing over our two karabiners on the wire to the side. Near the top it started raining and we followed a path down to the Dodici Apostoli Hut, arriving in mid afternoon.

Next day we were the last to leave the hut. We crossed a glacier, using our lightweight crampons, and found our via ferrata with stemples (metal steps) and wire cable zigzagging to a col. It was quite straightforward and our slings and karabiners made it feel very secure, even where exposed. The mist beat us to the col and we took a path with some ladders down to the Agostini Hut.

Once again, during the afternoon the hut was shrouded in damp, cold mist and it rained in the night.

We woke to find fresh snow outside the hut. The weather was slow to clear and we sat around on the hard wooden boards in the common room, finally leaving, after a good lunch, to walk back to the Pedrotti Hut. Jay was thrilled by the flowers, which were better than expected so late in the season, and everywhere the scenery was spectacular.

There was a fine sunrise next morning, with clouds in the valley, but outside the hut it felt cold. We decided to 'have a look' at the Sentiero delle Bochette and after breakfast walked up to the impressive Bocca di Brenta, framed by its vertical cliffs. The descent on the far side, on loose scree, caused problems for Jay's knees but luckily it wasn't far to the start of the route. The first ledges were dry so we continued. There was great exposure to our left and the views of the Crozzon di Brenta were fabulous. Some sections had no chains and needed considerable care, and sometimes the headroom was limited.

The route wound around the Cima Brenta Alta, and some scrambling, mostly without chains, led to the col below the Campanile Basso. It was quite misty on the east side. With more scrambling than I had expected, it was important to take care with route-finding. One very spectacular section led round the east side of the Torre di Brenta, with extraordinary exposure to the right. As a route, it certainly allows average mountaineers a glimpse of the world of the big-wall climber. Finally, a series of four ladders led down to the glacier. We had taken four hours and only passed three parties heading in the opposite direction.

Easy walking led down the glacier to the Alimonta Hut, where we enjoyed a beer and lunch before continuing around to the Brentei Hut. This hut was older and more traditional than others and, for once, we had a glorious sunny afternoon. We sat outside by the chapel, taking in the great views up to the Bocca di Brenta and feeling very pleased to have had such a sensational day on the Sentiero delle Bochette.

Next morning, we walked up the Val di Brenta and descended on the far side, making our way back towards Molveno down pleasant, grassy valleys and then through rather gloomy forests. Our friendly hotelier at the Hotel Gloria told us, rightly, that we had returned 'much richer through experience'. We decided to stay one extra day in Molveno. A chairlift took us to 1525m, where there was a great view of the Brenta Dolomites, and we had a pleasant day walk, with light sacks, to the summit of Croz dell' Altissimo. It was a peak which had looked very spectacular from our balcony and was a good end to our visit. Next day, we headed off to the Ortler, the next range to the north-west.

The Brenta Dolomites from above Molveno.

On the Sentiero delle Bochette. *Photo: J. Turner.*

Rhaetian Poppy.

Jay on the Sentiero delle Bochette.

Adamello and Presanella

Looking west from the Brenta Dolomites, our eyes were drawn to a pair of attractive snow summits, Monte Adamello and Cima Presanella. These mountains are formed from granitic rock and the area is therefore very different from the Brenta, with icefields, glaciers and deep, glacial valleys. It is a much quieter range and little known to British walkers and climbers. Jay and I returned to Italy in 2008 to visit the area and, hopefully, climb the two major summits.

We started at Carisolo, which we reached by hire car from Verona. Our warm-up day above Madonna di Campiglio was rather unsuccessful: it rained and I lost my glasses when they fell from what I thought was a pocket in my new anorak. The next day was altogether better. We drove up the Val Genova, a deep valley with rock slabs and steep pine woods on each side, and jagged ridges above, and passed a fine waterfall, Cascade di Nardis. The more open, upper part of the valley with its pastures was also very beautiful. From the last car park, we set off for the Mandrone Hut.

The path climbed steeply through the wood and there were plentiful wildflowers, including lilies and orchids. Above the trees, the path continued more gently, giving us fine views of the glacier opposite, with steep rock slabs and a waterfall below. The hut was quiet, standing just above some lovely tarns, and in the evening we had a good view of Cima Presanella. I felt very happy to be back at an Alpine hut. From our dormitory we could hear the roar of the glacial torrent across the valley.

Next day, boulder-hopping over rough ground, we clambered up to a col, Passo Payer (2978m). The rocks were formed of distinctive Tonalite, black and white, with rectangular hornblende crystals. To reach the col, we crossed some snow patches and scrambled up a short gully past some bright gentians. In the afternoon, we descended to the valley and, the day after, moved round to the Val Nambrone, where we drove up a single-track road with a series of zigzags from 1300m to 1900m. From a parking place at the top of the zigzags, we followed the path to the Segantini Hut.

We set off at 5.00 the next morning to attempt Cima Presanella, taking a steep, rocky path above the hut. As we gained height, the mist thinned to reveal a dramatic rock spire above. The path traversed below some crags and we had some awkward clambering over blocks and the odd snow patch before climbing steeply to the Passo dei Quattro Cantoni (2809m). There were lovely gentians and saxifrage on the slopes and a magnificent view, framed by rock cliffs, of the Brenta Dolomites above a sea of cloud.

The next kilometre and a half, crossing boulder fields, was very slow going but we passed some attractive clumps of glacier crowfoot. Long snow slopes then led up towards Cima Presanella, with a rock band near the top. Unfortunately, the rock band involved some awkward, loose rock and ice and, as Jay's knees were already suffering from the rough ground below, she decided not to continue. I went on to the very large summit cross before returning to Jay who, I think, was glad of a rest. We returned by the same route; it had been quite a tiring day.

We descended to the valley next morning and drove round to Val di Sole in the rain. The following day we continued over the Passo del Tonale and, passing through Edolo, headed south down the Val Camonica, in more rain, aiming to approach Adamello from the south-west. We turned off the main road at Berzo-Demo, two villages perched on a steep, wooded hillside. At Cevo we got a soaking as we ran to the little shop in a thunderstorm. Beyond the final village, Saviore, we drove 2.5km up the hill on a narrow, single-track road to the Stella Alpina refuge. In a torrential thunderstorm and with a misted windscreen, this was a 'character-building' drive, especially crossing one rough stream bed below a waterfall. I was profoundly grateful that we met no vehicles coming down. The refuge was a cheerful place. We were the only people staying and, despite the usual language problems, we managed to secure a reasonable supper.

In the morning, we walked in sunlight up the attractive valley, past the Lago di Salerno, to the Prudenzini Hut, where the hut warden had a friendly Nepalese assistant who spoke some English. The next day's climb to access the glacier below Monte Adamello looked a long way. We set off at 5.15am, first passing meadows and braided streams behind the hut. Though the path then climbed steeply, it was easy going compared to the path to Passo dei Quattro Cantoni on Presanella. After two hours, we reached hard snow, and cramponed up steep slopes, following old tracks to reach the glacier and a fine view of Adamello.

We crossed the glacier, heading to the south-west ridge, which appeared to have the gentler angle. At the ridge, we climbed, mostly over broken rocks and then some snow, to reach the summit, a large block of rock requiring a mantelshelf move. There was a bell below the small cross and distant views of Cima Presanella but we didn't linger long as cloud was building up. Luckily, we managed to retrace our faint track across the glacier as clouds drifted in and out, making strange shadows on the snow.

We got back to the hut after a very satisfying ten-and-a-half-hour day and, in the morning, went back down to the Stella Alpina. There was a sign saying *Strada Chiuso* but there are worse places to be stuck than in bright Alpine sun with fine views down the valley. Eventually, we followed another car down at lunchtime, moving a few rocks to cross the stream bed. The following day, we walked to the Tita Secchi Hut for lunch and ended our holiday with a visit to the tourist resort of Sirmeone on Lake Garda.

Rock spire below Cima Presanella.

Jay on the glacier below Monte Adamello.

Flowers of the Adamello and Presanella area:

Creeping Avens;

Rough Saxifrage;

Rhaetian Rampion;

Moss Campion and King of the Alps;

St Bruno's Lily.

TWENTY FIVE

Ski-tours

Ski-touring is a wonderful way of travelling through the mountains in winter. Moving uphill is rhythmical and breaking trail in fresh snow can be very aesthetic, while skiing downhill on perfect powder can be totally exhilarating. In the Alps, the network of huts allows rucksacks to be kept to a reasonable weight, although the huts get crowded at peak periods. Ski-touring can, however, be more serious than summer climbing due to the dangers of crevasses, avalanches and exposed icy slopes.

During the 1980s, most of my ski-touring was in the Pyrenees and the mountains of Spain but, after my return to Britain from the Far East in 1993, I made up for lost time in the Alps. In April that year, I spent an enjoyable week in the Oetztal with Mike Daly and Jos Widdershoven, climbing several summits. A month later, I led a small party on the Italian High Level Route. We climbed the Breithorn and Pollux before bad weather forced a difficult descent from the Upper Mezzalama Hut.

I continued to ski-tour in the Alps most years, usually with Jay, on Eagle Ski Club trips. Unguided tours were the most memorable and included good weeks in the Ortler, led by Peter Lancaster, and in the Oberland, Kleinwalsertal and Stubai, led by Mike Hendry. Jay was President of the Eagle Ski Club from 2006-2009 and one of our last Alpine tours together was a trip, led by Steve Goulden, in the Queyras, a delightful area for ski-touring.

Jay and I also attended Alpine Ski Club meets based in Andermatt and Briançon. Both venues have very good day tours in the surrounding area. In addition, we spent a week at Mürren during the Club's centenary celebrations in 2008.

Unfortunately, not all my tours have been free of accidents and tragedy. My last tour with John Harding was a disastrous trip to the Monte Viso area, when John's friend Alan Wedgwood was very seriously hurt in a small fall and had to be rescued by helicopter; and in 2004 I returned early from the Alpine

Ski Club expedition to Turkey after the death of Alastair Ross in an avalanche at Palandöken.

The rest of this chapter describes three ski-tours which have given particular pleasure in recent years, two in the Alps and one in Arctic Norway.

Mont Blanc

At 1.30pm on 4th May 2006, Ken White and I stood with our skis on the summit of Mont Blanc, looking out in perfect weather on the extensive vista of mountain ranges. For me, having failed to climb Mont Blanc during Jeremy Whitehead's tour in 1986 and again with John Evans in 1996, this was definitely a case of 'third time lucky'.

We had organized the logistics through Nick Parks, with a comfortable chalet in Argentière and a young, bearded, French guide, François Peyron. I was already fit from a tour in the Stubai and Ken had spent two days touring and acclimatizing in the area before I arrived. The day before our ascent, we woke to a beautiful spring morning and a wonderful view of Mont Blanc from our chalet. François took us skiing above Argentière, hurtling down the glacier on some very steep, icy runs. I was frightened of hurting myself before Mont Blanc but somehow managed to avoid falling.

Back in the village, under a sun umbrella in 22°C heat, we had an excellent omelette Savoyarde for lunch. Later that afternoon, after François had been through Ken's rucksack, throwing out all excess weight such as penknife and sheet sleeping bag, we caught the 4.30 téléphérique to the Aiguille du Midi. At the top, we put on harness and crampons before descending the snow arête, our guide bouncing like a puppy in front. There were great views across to the Grandes Jorasses but suspicious banks of cloud on the Italian side. A quick ski below the south face of the Aiguille du Midi and a short uphill carry led to the Cosmiques Hut.

The hut provided breakfast options at 1.00, 3.00 or 5.00. François chose the late option. I didn't sleep a wink, what with the excitement and the noise of others getting up all through the night. By the time we set off at 5.45, there was already a lovely orange glow over the mountains to the east. We skinned up the slopes of Mont Blanc du Tacul. It felt quite exposed and I was glad of the added security of *harscheisen*; for one very steep section we took off our skis to climb on foot. The sun arrived on the face, lighting the seracs, and I was pleased we had not started earlier and done the climb by torchlight.

The track zigzagged between seracs and crevasses and the climb was longer than I had expected but eventually we reached the shoulder, not far from the summit. We kept skins on our skis for a gentle, downhill track into the basin below Mont Maudit. From below, the crux section looked quite intimidating. We shouldered skis. The sacks felt far too heavy, the sun was hot, and it seemed very hard work zigzagging up Mont Maudit on crampons, roped together. Crossing the bergschrund involved a very difficult move, putting one crampon above waist-height and pulling hard on an axe in soft snow. The steep section above was protected by partly buried fixed ropes.

From the shoulder of Mont Maudit, we cramponed slightly downhill to the Col de la Brenva. We could see Mont Blanc in front now, in clear blue skies criss-crossed with vapour trails. We stopped for some food but I was too thirsty to eat much. Then we shouldered our horribly heavy packs and continued on foot up the steep, icy slopes of the Mur de la Côte. Despite the effort of carrying skis at altitude, I realized that we were definitely going to make it, and for a short time I felt quite emotional about achieving such a long-desired objective.

François set a demanding pace, sometimes modified by Ken stopping to pant for a few breaths. We made several detours on to the north face to check snow conditions for the descent and even overtook a couple of Austrian guides. At the top, there were about fifteen people in a spacious area below the summit. It was extraordinary to stand there, taking photographs, without even wearing an anorak.

I was far from relaxed during the thirty minutes we spent up there, knowing that François planned to ski down the north face, which is 40 degrees at the top. He assured us that we would have 'the ski run of our lives'. We skied straight from the summit and, after a few icy traverses, found the snow had softened just enough to give exhilarating skiing down a long, steep slope. As we lost height, the scenery became truly spectacular as we passed between crevasses – one of which we jumped – and below large ice cliffs, where it was necessary to ski fast to avoid the risk of falling ice.

Once on the ordinary route, the skiing was easier as there was a semi-piste. I was very tired and made use of long traverses where possible. The scenery was extremely impressive but long sections of the route were threatened by potential serac-fall and I could see why guides no longer like to ascend by this route. It was a long ski down to the Grand Mulets Hut, taking rests where we could find safe spots.

We stopped in a hollow below the hut, feeling utterly exhausted. François argued strongly for going on down to Chamonix, claiming 'La Jonction' would be icy in the morning and adding the incentives of showers and a comfortable bed. But the deciding factor was that to reach the hut required climbing about 100m of ladders. We skied on down in soft snow, followed by a scruffy, young French pair from Briançon, one on a snowboard and the other on Nordic skis, with their Alsatian dog, equipped with its own snow goggles.

The route through the crevasses and seracs of the Bossons Glacier was quite straightforward; we had some side-stepping at the start and then a gentle downhill trail. Once on the other side, we put on skins for a slight ascent and a long traversing path across the avalanche-prone slopes below the Aiguille de Midi. It was 5.00pm when we reached the téléphérique station and the lady let us pile into a fairly full cabin without buying a ticket. At Chamonix, we waited in the hot sun while François fetched his car. There was nowhere nearby to buy a drink. It felt very strange to have descended so fast.

On Mont Blanc du Tacul.

Mont Blanc from Mont Blanc du Tacul. Still a long way to go! *Photo: K. White.*

On the summit of Mont Blanc. *Photo: K. White.*

Ecrins

In April 2007, I flew out to Grenoble for a week's ski-mountaineering in the Ecrins. The tour was arranged by the Eagle Ski Club and there were just three of us and a guide, Rick Marchant from Chamonix. The Ecrins have a reputation for serious ski-mountaineering, and the tour description used terms such as 'challenging' and 'a very physical week', so, when Rick told us at dinner on the first night, in La Grave, that he had warmed up by climbing the North Face of the Eiger the preceding week, I had a suspicion that the week might be a bit different from normal ski-touring.

Apprehension was further heightened by observing a helicopter rescue of an injured skier from the slopes above the Châtelleret Hut on the first day. We went up to the hut from La Bérarde, rather than skiing over from La Grave, due to concerns about snow conditions in the hot afternoon sun. Next morning we climbed hard frozen snow on skins and *harscheisen* to the Col de la Casse Déserte. This was an intimidating, steep climb where the penalty for dropping a piece of equipment or, worse still, missing a kick-turn was not to be considered. We climbed two sections on crampons and the col itself, a dramatic gash between impressive rock walls, was crossed on crampons both up and down. After a very short descent, we climbed on foot up to the Col des Neiges, then a short ski down led to the Refuge Adèle Planchard (3169m), high enough for, in my case, a slight altitude headache.

Next morning, we enjoyed a fine Alpine dawn as we climbed up to the summit of La Grande Ruine (Pointe Brevoort, 3765m) on skins at first, and then crampons. The summit was a magnificent viewpoint and we had a great ski descent down the Glacier de la Plate des Agneaux, below the impressive rock walls of Roche d'Alvau and Roche Faurio, to the Refuge de l'Alpe de Villar d'Arène. The hut was low enough for the luxury of running water and even showers. My diary entry that evening reads: 'Tomorrow we have a 4.00am start, a 1600m climb, a terrifying traverse and a 30m abseil.'

So it proved! We skinned up the valley by torchlight and continued towards our objective, Pic de Neige Cordier (3614m), in early morning sunlight. A steep 200m couloir gave access to the north ridge, which we climbed partly on foot and partly on skins, before a few pitches of roped climbing led to the summit, another great viewpoint. The 'terrifying traverse' to the Col Pic Emile wasn't too bad, but the abseil down steep, loose rock with heavy skis on our packs was certainly thought-provoking. After replacing our skis while still hanging on the abseil rope, assisted by the guide, we side-slipped, then skied down to the Glacier Blanc and on down to the Refuge du Glacier Blanc.

The next day, we again got up at 4.00am, with the aim of climbing the Barre or Dôme des Ecrins. We cramponed up the slopes behind the hut and then skinned up the Glacier Blanc, arriving below the face in good time, but decided that the route was unjustifiably exposed to icefall danger from seracs. Instead, we turned right and climbed up Roche Faurio (3730m), with great views of Barre des Ecrins behind. The summit had a sting in its tail, requiring a few pitches, in ski-boots and crampons, of PD rock climbing in an extremely exposed situation.

The plan on our last day was to climb to the Col du Monêtier (3339m) and ski down to le Monêtier-les-Bains. I was naively concerned that this might be an anticlimax. Wrong! The climb up to the col had an extremely steep section, which we tackled on skis and *harscheisen*, but later decided would have been safer on crampons. Above, an interesting climb on foot led to the col and a stunning view, looking east towards Italy and a huge arc of the Alps, and back west to Mont Pelvoux and L'Ailefroide. Part of the descent was equally steep and still icy – not a place to fall – before we could ski on down a fine valley. The snow became increasingly difficult and ran out at about 1800m. Finally, we walked through larch forests and meadows down to the town and a well-deserved beer and lunch.

Magnificent mountains, perfect weather, a very strong team and a good guide had all combined to give a strenuous and memorable week of serious ski-mountaineering.

Steve Day rock climbing in ski boots on Roche Faurio.

Ian Scorah on Roche Faurio, Barre des Ecrins behind.

Lyngen

After skiing down the north face of Mont Blanc and participating in an exceptionally good ski-tour in the Ecrins the following year, there was a risk that another Alpine tour might be an anticlimax. The answer was to try a new area and, influenced by reports from fellow Eagle Ski Club members and pictures on the internet, I decided to organize an Eagle Ski Club tour to the Lyngen Alps in Arctic Norway for 2009.

The Lyngen peninsular is situated about 50km east of Tromsø and consists of steep, glaciated mountains rising straight from the sea. Snow lies down to sea level until April each year. For our visit, we were based at Lyngen Lodge, on the east side of Lyngen Fjord, where the mountains are more amenable for ski-touring. The Lodge has a great view across the fjord to the Lyngen Alps. It is owned and run by a British guide, Graham Austick, and his Norwegian partner and provides very comfortable accommodation and excellent catering. The great advantage of staying at Lyngen Lodge is that they provide a powerful speedboat for access to ski-tours. A slight disadvantage is that only guided touring is allowed.

The team consisted of David Seddon, Paul Miller, Declan Phelan, Philippa Cockman, Christine Watkins, Jay and me. We flew from Gatwick to Tromsø, with superb views of the Norwegian mountains and coast, especially the snow-covered Lofoten Islands. Transferring from Tromsø to Lyngen Lodge by minibus, we noticed groups of locals fishing through holes in the ice on the frozen fjords.

On our first day we used the boat to speed north up the Lyngen Fjord to Uløya Island. At Havnnes, we inspected racks of cod, which are air-dried for about three months and then salted. We then skinned up Kjelvågtinden (1034m) in soft snow. The summit was in cloud but we had excellent powder-snow skiing on the descent with a great light on the fjord below. The last 200m to the beach, through dense silver birch trees were quite challenging. We were picked up by rubber dinghy and transferred back to the boat for the return trip to the Lodge. From the boat, in the late afternoon sun, we took photographs of the steep wall of peaks on the west side of Lyngen Fjord.

Next day, the weather was perfect and we had a great ski tour up Stortinden (1077m), followed by a good powder descent. Another 400m climb took us to a col before we descended a valley with long schusses towards the lowering sun. We felt tired after 1500m of climbing but very satisfied after an excellent tour. Our third day was the best. We returned to Uløya Island and made an east-west traverse, climbing Blåtinden (1142m) with marvellous views past snowy mountains to the blue waters of the Barents Sea and across to the spectacular Lyngen Alps. The skiing from the summit in powder snow was as good as any I could remember and we had more good skiing next day on Gillavarri (1163m).

The day after, we took the boat to cross Lyngen Fjord, put on our skis on the edge of the beach and skinned up a long glacier to Tafeltinden (1385m). Under grey skies, the tour lacked some of the magic of the previous days. Our last trip was a traverse of Kågen Island, again under grey skies in warm temperatures. We didn't climb the high peaks due to avalanche danger but our Austrian guide, Paul Held, claimed that in good weather the ski-mountaineering on Kågen Island is as good as anywhere in the world.

As with all mountaineering and ski-mountaineering, the success of a trip depends on the weather. We were lucky in Lyngen. There is definitely a magic feeling about skiing above the sea, and this trip combined fabulous powder-snow skiing from summit to seashore with great scenery.

Lyngen Lodge.

Jay skiing just below the summit of Blåtinden.

Paul Miller skiing down Gillavarri.

Twenty Six

Scotland

At WesternGeco, my job is to initiate new seismic surveys offshore north-west Europe. The role requires close liaison with oil company clients and, as many of them are based in Aberdeen or Stavanger, Jay and I moved to Aberdeenshire in November 2002. We live only an hour and a half's drive from the heart of the Cairngorms National Park and there are many good walks on smaller hills locally. It's easy to become complacent and forget what a privilege it is to live in a country of such outstanding natural beauty.

On our arrival in Scotland, Jay had only about thirty-five Munros left to climb. Completing the remaining ones became an objective but never an obsession. We were able to collect some summits while attending Eagle Ski Club meets and to plan others for Easter weekends with our long-suffering friends Ken and Alison. Each August I gave Jay a Munro weekend as part of her birthday present.

After four years, Jay had about ten Munros left. We spent a few summer days at a bothy in gloomy Glen Dessary to collect some remote summits on the edge of Knoydart. We cycled into Culra Bothy on a hot summer day for Ben Alder, and we also used cycles to approach Gulvain from the north, having previously been blasted off the south summit by fierce winds. The problem of Beinn Fionnlaidh was solved by taking a boat on Loch Mullardoch, followed by a long walk over several summits in low cloud to get back to the dam.

Jay's final Munro was Ben More on Mull, in May 2008. We rented a fine lodge near the base of the mountain and invited thirty-five of our mountaineering friends, some staying at the lodge, some camping in the garden and others staying locally. On the appointed day, the weather was truly terrible, with rain lashing against the French windows of the lodge. It took the full force of the Ladies Scottish Climbing Club to persuade Jay to hold the celebration party but postpone the ascent until the next day. Fortunately they prevailed. We had a great dinner and next day we climbed Ben More via the A'Chioch ridge in perfect weather. The rest of the week was a wonderful West Coast holiday in the company of our good friends.

Inevitably, the years of helping Jay to complete the Munros meant that my own total steadily increased. When I was much younger, and a keen rock climber, I regarded hill walking as a boring way to spend a fine day. However, once I had climbed over 200 Munros, it seemed logical to complete the list. I have now climbed all but sixteen.

I confess to a love-hate relationship with Munros. They give the best of days, but occasionally also the worst. Inevitably, there have been days of bogs and unrelenting rain. Most recently, on a dreary plod to Beinn Mhanach with Ken White, every stitch of clothing was soaked by the time we returned to the car. However, the good days by far outnumber the bad ones. Living in Scotland and using modern weather forecasts it is easy to become a fair-weather mountaineer. For me, the pleasure is in the view and in photography, so I am generally happy to pick and choose the good days and walk in the glens during damp weather.

I must have spent the best part of a year of my life walking on Scottish hills, in all seasons. The variety is extraordinary. In just the last year, I have padded up the gabbro slabs of the Dubhs Ridge from Loch Coruisk on Skye in hot summer sun and walked up the rounded Ben Chonzie in Perthshire on a winter day, when there was so much ice we kept our crampons on all the way back to the car. Last November (2010) I skied to the summit of our local hill, Bennachie, and a week later, with my godson Rob Lowe, spent a superb day ski-touring on the Glenshee hills with snow right down to the road.

My last outing with Jay, before being diagnosed with cancer, was also near Glenshee on a cloudless January day. We walked up to the col between Cairn of Claise and Glas Maol, and as we descended steeply, using crampons, into Caenlochan Glen at the head of Glen Isla, the sunlight on the snow and ice around the rim of the corrie gave quite an 'alpine' feel to the place. We climbed up 'Banana Gully' beside Little Glas Maol and continued over the summit of Glas Maol before dropping down to the car.

Below, I have listed ten of my best days walking or ski-touring in Scotland. Like the earlier list of favourite climbs, it is completely subjective as so much depends on the weather and company. Making the choices was very difficult and it is interesting there is no room for Ben Nevis, Glencoe, Torridon, Glen Affric or even our local Munro, Lochnagar, which has given great days in winter and summer. The list is just a bit of fun for readers who enjoy Scottish hills.

Best Days in Scotland:

Grey Corries Ridge ski-tour	A ski-traverse on an Eagle Ski Club meet in 1986. A magnificent day, described in Chapter 9.
An Teallach	The finest mainland ridge in Britain, with some scrambling and great views. I first did this in snowy conditions in 1976 and repeated it with Jay in summer 1999.
Stob Binnein and Ben More ski tour.	Another memorable ski tour, with Ken White, described in an earlier chapter. A fine winter sunset from Ben More.
The 'Big Six'	Jay and I climbed these remote mountains in the heart of the Letterewe and Fisherfield wilderness area from a campsite near Shenaval in 2006. Outstanding views from Beinn Tarsuinn towards Slioch.
Clach Glas and Blaven	Some of the best scrambling on Skye. A great day with Jay. We used a short rope to protect one pitch on Blaven.
Suilven	My friends Robert Whitcombe and Philip Tibbs come to Scotland each year for a weekend's walking. I think this was our most enjoyable day, in perfect May weather.
Beinn Liath Mhor, Sgorr Ruadh and Fuar Tholl	A superb summer round with Jay in 2004. Sgorr Ruadh and Fuar Tholl are both spectacular peaks. Jay swam in a tarn between them.
Sgor an Lochain Uaine (Angel's Peak), Cairngorms.	An elegant ridge to a remote summit, climbed with Michael Vaughan in 1983 and described in Chapter 9.
Conival and Ben More Assynt	A very enjoyable summer walk with Robert Whitcombe, his son Charles and Richard Smith in 2003.
Beinn Tarsuinn – A'Chir ridge, Arran	I have always loved being on mountains near the sea and Arran is perfect in this respect. I did this enjoyable ridge walk with Richard Dowsett in 1979 and again with Jay in 1987.

Dave Howe on Sgurr nan Gillean.

On Mullach Coire Mhic Fhearchair during the 'big six' walk. *Photo: J. Turner.*

Suilven.

Lochnagar in April.

Ben Rinnes in snow at Easter 2010. Ben Rinnes is a Corbett near Dufftown which gives very good ski touring.

Blackrock Cottage, Glencoe.

Ken White and Alison Graham below Sgurr Choinnich Beag. Ken and Alison have been our companions on many Munros.

Epilogue

The operation to remove the tumour from my pancreas was unsuccessful. The surgeon found that the cancer had spread to my liver and, in this situation, the procedure is to terminate the operation. It means that my life expectancy, even with chemotherapy, is statistically only nine months although, being fit, I firmly intend to beat the average.

Naturally, a short lifespan focuses the mind on questions of God and religion. Although I have been reading about spiritual matters, I don't have easy answers. I no longer believe in a conventional Christian God. At the same time, I struggle with the idea that the universe, this planet, life and all the beauty in nature are a random accident.

Enjoyment of beauty has underpinned all the mountain travels described in this book. Some writers, like W H Murray, have expressed, with great eloquence, the concept that beauty in the mountains can raise one's awareness of a creator. I can sympathize with this idea, although it is unfashionable nowadays.

What is beauty? In *Mountains of the Mind*, Robert Macfarlane discusses how we are influenced by the writers and artists in the eighteenth and nineteenth centuries who developed the idea of 'the sublime'. However, although we are influenced by our upbringing, I also think that we are born with an ability to appreciate beauty. Of course, beauty is not restricted to mountains, or even to nature. It can be found in art, music, architecture everywhere, even in science, but mountains are where it is most obvious to me. Crossing glaciers in the early dawn, as an orange glow spreads behind a jagged rock ridge, are some of the moments when I have felt most fully alive.

I was inspired to try mountaineering by reading R L G Irving's *The Romance of Mountaineering*. I hope that my book can likewise inspire at least one teenager to find similar joy and beauty in the mountains. I also very much hope I have been able to bring back good memories for my many friends who have shared days in the hills.

Glossary

Abseil	Descend by sliding down the rope
Belay	Tie oneself to the rock
Bergschrund	A large crevasse between a glacier and the rock above

Climbing Grades	*In the UK, rock climbs are graded:*	*In the Alps, routes are graded:*
	Moderate (Mod)	Facile (F)
	Difficult (Diff)	Peu Difficile (PD)
	Very Difficult (V Diff)	Assez Difficile (AD)
	Severe (S)	Difficile (D)
	Very Severe (VS)	Extremement Difficile (ED)
	Hard Very Severe (HVS)	
	Extremely Severe (XS)	

Gendarme	Rock tower on a ridge
Glissade	Slide down snow in a standing position
Gripped	Frozen with fear on a rock climb
Harscheisen	Ski crampons
Karabiner	Metal snap link
Pitch	Rope length
Runner	Running belay. Usually a nut placed in a crack in the rock. The rope then passes through a karabiner attached to the nut.
Serac	Ice cliff
V Diff	See 'Climbing Grades'
Verglass	Ice glaze on rock
Via Ferrata	A path equipped with ladders and safety wire
VS	See 'Climbing Grades'
Zawn	A narrow inlet in a sea cliff

A Note on
Photography

Photography is very important to me. It is my way of trying to capture and share some of the beauty I find in the mountains and elsewhere. With the exception of a photograph of me in Arctic Norway by Patrick Bermingham and two pictures of our Mont Blanc trip by Ken White, I took all the photographs in this book apart from those which include me, which were taken with my camera. These are acknowledged wherever possible. I am more interested in the results than the technology, but for readers who would like details, they are as follows.

The first photograph, at Swanage, was taken with a small instamatic camera and I have scanned the print. While still at Winchester, I bought a Kodak 35mm camera and I started using transparencies before the trip to Arctic Norway in 1977.

I bought a Minota XG2 SLR camera before the trip to Nepal and kept with Minolta XG2 or XG-300 cameras until 2006, although one broke and one was lost in Indonesia. I think that all the pictures in this book from that time were taken with a standard 50mm lens. I also had a zoom lens but it was too heavy to carry up mountains. I nearly always used automatic exposure settings, although I often increased the aperture by one or two stops when taking photographs on snow. I always used a skylight filter.

I generally used Kodachome 25 or 64 transparencies, occasionally Agfa, and for the New Zealand trip I used Fuji Velvia film. All gave good results and the transparencies have lasted, in some cases over 35 years, with no apparent deterioration. Once I moved to the Far East in 1990, I started using print film rather than transparencies, as it was more practical, but I still used transparencies for major trips.

I finally went digital in 2006, after one print film was lost (it was found two years later in a drawer in the post room at work) and disappointment with my Mont Blanc transparencies. I bought a small Canon IXUS camera. I soon lost the first one, which fell down Eagle Ridge on Lochnagar; the camera is now carried on a cord round my neck and the case is also tied on. A second one broke just before a holiday and I am now on my third, a Canon IXUS 970 IS. The lens is not as good as an SLR camera lens but the small weight and size, and the convenience of being able to zoom, more than compensate. The camera has a good screen and I enjoy reviewing my pictures each evening.

To reproduce photographs for this book, I needed to scan transparencies and a few negatives, so I bought an Epson Perfection V500 flatbed scanner. I have mostly scanned at 400 dpi and I use the supplied 'digital ICE technology' for removing dust. I touched up the odd remaining blemish using Adobe Photoshop software which was supplied with the scanner. Initially I was very happy with the results but close inspection revealed some fringing problems and many transparencies were re-scanned professionally.

Acknowledgements

I wish to thank the following for their help, support and encouragement with this book:

Stephen Goodwin, editor of the Alpine Club Journal, and Mike and Jenny Spencer, editors of the Eagle Ski Club Yearbook, for permission to use previously published material; Granta Books for permission to use the quote from *Mountains of the Mind*.

John Harding, Stephanie Macdonald, Margaret Clennett, Ken Wilson and Stephen Goodwin for help finding potential publishers; Derek Fordham, John Gunner, Jeremy Whitehead and my wife Jay for help with the editing; Vivien Cripps, at Millrace, for professional editing and great encouragement and support.

Jon Barton and his team at Vertebrate Publishing for their professional service.

And, my special thanks to Jay for looking after me during my illness while I have been writing.